ROCK YOUR BUSINESS

26 Essential Lessons to Help You Plan, Run, and Grow Your New Business from the Ground Up

BONI WAGNER-STAFFORD
JOHN WAGNER-STAFFORD

Ingenium
Books

Published by Ingenium Books Publishing

Toronto, Ontario, Canada M6P 1Z2

www.ingeniumbooks.com

Cover Design by Jessica Bell Designs

ISBN: 978-1-989059-07-4 (paperback/softcover)

978-1-989059-06-7 (electronic)

978-1-989059-08-1 (hardcover/hardback)

978-1-989059-01-2 (audiobook)

To Morgan, Clara and Ella

Contents

Introduction

We applaud your independent nature. Whether you're an entrepreneur, you run your own small business, you're self-employed, or you're an iPro, you're a driving force in today's global economy. You work out how to get things done better, faster, with new approaches, tools, markets, or technology. You drive innovation, create jobs, and spur global economic growth.

You show the world that it IS possible; that conformity and convention are not always a good thing. You take responsibility, accept the consequences, rise above failures, and make the world a better place.

In *Rock Your Business*, we explore what it's all about to work for yourself rather than someone else. We look at how to figure out what that work is and who might benefit from your new business idea. We talk about locking in your *why* and using your purpose to set yourself apart from your competitors. We broach the legal matters you're advised to consider and open the door to peek into business structures. We touch on intellectual property, setting up systems, and we reveal an approach to getting the right team on board.

We also peel back the curtain on culture and discuss opportunities to put culture to work for you, rather than against. We count the pennies in cash flow management and share some tips on leveraging technology in everyday administration. We even show you ways to ensure you're getting the most out of meetings.

We help you decide whether you wish to grow your business, and, if so, we present a few ideas on how to do it. We share some resources to help you improve productivity. And we give you permission to ditch the clients that are just plain bad for your business.

We provide some guidelines for you to ensure you're creating brand content that truly connects with your customers and clients to draw them in. We touch on marketing and trade shows and signs you might be ready to sell or exit your business. We suggest ways that writing a book might be good for your business. And, because we're all about balance, we help you look for signposts that you need to build in some more downtime to ensure you can keep giving your business your best.

The Daring and the Drive

Being an entrepreneur and in business for yourself is an exhilarating ride. Whether you're starting up with a unique business idea, developing a new technological solution to an everyday problem, or buying and operating a franchise, there's a lot to juggle in the planning, execution, and measurement. It takes a bit of science, a lot of instinct, and some tried and true steps and approaches to follow on the pathway to success.

Those of us with the daring and the drive to go solo are kicking up kudos in the global economy. In a 2016 global job creation survey of entrepreneurs by EY (formerly known as Ernst & Young), 59 per cent said they planned to expand their workforces and hire, while only 28 per cent of large corporations planned to grow.

That means entrepreneur-led companies are twice as likely to grow as their big business counterparts.

The Value of Self-education

Education is important in entrepreneurial endeavours, as it is for any other career pursuit. There is a correlation between education level and salary, for example. But education systems are still playing catchup to the mindsets of millennials. The generation that values autonomy and freedom above almost all else is more entrepreneurial than any generation before.

According to a 2014 U.S. survey, conducted jointly by Buzz Marketing Group and the Young Entrepreneurship Council, 93 per cent of the respondents believe entrepreneurial education is important, but only 38 per cent had ever been given a chance at one. Yes, you can go to college or university and obtain your MBA (Master of Business Administration); however, three thoughts emerge for us here:

1. Book learning is only one part of a business education.
2. Not everyone has the opportunity or desire to pursue a business degree.
3. Entrepreneurship, self-employment and freelancing tend to be solitary endeavours.

It helps to talk to other people, hear how others have handled a similar challenge or situation, and to read about the successes of others. That's what this book is for.

What we discuss in this book are simplified concepts you can spend thousands of dollars to read about hypothetically in business school. We share our own stories, as well as the real life stories of other everyday entrepreneurs who have been there, done that.

Read a chapter or two at bedtime. Read the whole thing cover to cover in one sitting. The information is easy to absorb. *Rock Your Business* is a great accompaniment to your experience and education.

The Roots of Rock Your Business

Rock Your Business is born out of our own experience (co-authors Boni and John) running small businesses, working freelance, contributing to leadership teams in the startup and growth phases of small businesses as well as in public and private sector corporations.

Throughout our careers, independently and together, we've been through the set up, the learning curve, the systems, the website building, the blog writing, the social media marketing (and, yes, you will get clients from your social media activities), the legal, the planning, the prospecting, the selling, the visioning and purpose, the technical requirements... and more.

We've learned, we've failed, and we've succeeded. We understand how much we can still learn from the experience of others – and how much we learn and benefit from failures.

We've experienced a common thread. Whether you call us freelancers, self-employed, or entrepreneurs doesn't matter. From the geographical freedom of our 40' sailboat, *Ingenium*, we do the kind of work we love for clients we enjoy. We have no one but ourselves to report to, call to task, praise, discipline, or collaborate with on decision making.

Which is something we sometimes want. And that's what we're doing with *Rock Your Business*. We are providing a way for you to connect with the real life stories of other people in the same situation as you.

Rock Your Business will give you the information and real life examples to help ensure any stepping-stone failures are little ones that pave the way to your big successes and not the big boulders that block your way.

Follow the suggestions, advice and guidelines in this book and you will have what it takes to *Rock Your Business*.

STEP 1

The Groundwork

The Geology of Business

> *Geology: a science that deals with the earth's physical structure and substance, its history, and the processes that act on it.*

The way we all work is changing – because of technology, a globalized economy, and business evolution. Our fathers – Mr. Wagner and Mr. Stafford – each worked for one employer for the bulk of their careers. Our mothers bridged that gap between doing the 'right' thing, which for a time was staying home with the kids, and doing what fulfilled them. That was, at various times and for each of them, owning and operating a store and working in the management ranks of a major Canadian telecommunications company.

In our parents' day, it was expected and common to have a single employer, if not a single career. Today, not so much. About 15 years ago, a person could expect to have five careers in his or her lifetime. Today?

In Canada, more people were self-employed in 2016 (nearly 2.8 million) than at any time in the previous 30 years. The OECD

(Organization for Economic Cooperation & Development) reports self-employment rates from 2015 as a percentage of total employment as follows:

- The United States 6.5%
- Canada 8.6%
- Australia 10.3%
- Germany 10.8%
- Japan 11.1%
- United Kingdom 14.9%
- European Union (28 countries) 16.1%
- Italy 24.7%

Entrepreneurs ask questions, challenge the status quo, compete successfully against "traditional" companies and come up with new processes and products that drive innovation.

The Freelancing Boom

Freelancing is also now big business. In the United States, 53 million people or 34 per cent of the workforce report doing freelance work. In the U.K., it is estimated that there are 1.4 million freelancers and growing. Across the European Union, the shifting trend of moving from having a job to working directly for clients has shown explosive growth. Independent professionals, or iPros as we call them, represent the only growing segment of the labour market and a significant positive economic force in post-recession Europe.

These iPros represent 25 per cent of the workforce in professional, scientific and technical roles, and 22 per cent of all workers in arts and entertainment.

Standard employment is either unavailable or discarded as an option because of the requirement for conformity and the resultant smothering of creativity. More than a third (37 per cent) of E.U. citizens responding to a survey indicated they prefer to work independently, but they are held back by red tape, perceived lack of funding and skills, and a fear of failure.

In a research study called *Future Working: The Rise of Europe's Independent Professionals*, author Patricia Leighton says, "There is a scarcity of support for those starting out as an iPro. The perceived unavailability of relevant and affordable information and advice has resulted in iPros being concerned with their lack of business skills."

Surveys in both the U.S. and Canada suggest that by 2020 nearly half of the workforce will be comprised of freelancers, temporary, contract and on-call workers. Fifty per cent! When you combine the self-employed, the entrepreneurs who incorporate, and the freelancer or iPro cohort, this represents a significant economic shift.

This means that the majority of the workforce needs – or will soon need – some understanding of how to run a business. Because their livelihood depends on it.

Let's talk about the differences – and the similarities – between the iPro, the freelancer, the self-employed, and the small business entrepreneur. Which one(s) are you?

IPro

These independent professionals are individuals who are highly skilled, work for themselves, and do not employ others. They typically function in the rapid-paced knowledge economy and are a distinct group: they are classified neither as small business nor as entrepreneurs.

Freelancer

Today's freelancers may or may not be highly educated or highly skilled, but will provide their services to others independent of an employer. They may also contract pieces of work outside their skill set such as web design, bookkeeping, etcetera, to other freelancers or iPros. A freelancer likely won't have a business name registered with the relevant government body, and will likely file taxes as an individual while claiming some business expenses.

Self-employed

Those who are self-employed likely have a sole proprietorship or simple partnership business registered in order to add credibility and assist marketing efforts. Rarely will the self-employed hire others to work in the business, except for the service providers mentioned above.

Small Business Entrepreneur

These go-getters are tuned into market trends and gaps and work to capitalize on being first-to-market with a new idea, product, service, or technology. We would argue that some small business ventures are run by the self-employed and some self-employed people run small businesses. A small business that is incorporated becomes its own legal entity. And the entrepreneurs who run these incorporated small businesses are technically not self-employed; they are employed by the corporations they created.

The Small Business Numbers

In Canada, a small business is technically defined as having fewer than 100 employees. The Australian Bureau of Statistics defines a small business as having fewer than 20 employees. In the U.K. it's considered a small or medium-sized business if it has 250 or fewer employees. Depending on how you look at things in the U.S., 99.7 per cent of all firms classify as small business. But that's because the U.S. has an overly complicated classification system that changes the definition of small business industry by industry. It could have 500, 1000 or 1500 employees and still be considered a small business. Yeesh.

What these independent activists – freelancer, iPro, small business owner or entrepreneur – have in common is that they are *running businesses*. Size doesn't matter for that definition.

Entrepreneurs start businesses hoping they'll grow into the next Facebook. Small business owners work to provide a decent living and lifestyle for themselves and their families. Freelancers and iPros want the freedom to do the work they love for clients who appreciate their talents.

All of them are running businesses. They are all relatively solo endeavours, where there often isn't much time to connect with others who are working out the same kinks and learning the same tricks.

Regardless which category yours falls into, you bill clients directly, manage your own startup and sales and marketing and productivity and hiring and taxes and technology and... well, everything.

In addition to being awesome at what you do for clients, you must also become a quick study in the details of your business. It can be helpful to hear and read the stories of others... perhaps just before bed, where the ideas can percolate into your subconscious while you sleep, readying you to reach greater heights tomorrow.

2

Diamond or Coal
ATTITUDE & BELIEFS

> *Our beliefs control our bodies, our minds, and thus our lives...*
>
> Bruce Lipton, The Biology of Belief

A ttitude = altitude. It's as simple as that. Your attitude and your beliefs can either hold you back or propel you forward. Do you see a chunk of coal in the palm of your hand or a future diamond? Now, contrary to popular belief, coal is not a direct source in the formation of diamonds. They are simply different forms of carbon. We're sure you've got the analogy, though: how you look at things comprises your attitude.

Remember those people in the E.U. from chapter one who responded to the survey saying they wanted to work independently, but *feared failure*? They also worried they didn't have the skillset and didn't have the money to get started as an iPro. Those are the people who will likely never make a change because they have a prevailing belief, or attitude, of fear and unworthiness.

Fabian Dewar

Fabian was looking for a change after twenty years as a public sector manager. When an opportunity presented itself to buy a thriving online marketing business, Fabian went for it. He hired the right lawyers, the right accountants, and felt good about the meetings with the outgoing owners. Buying this business came with a catch: the package deal included a partner who would retain ownership of a 49 per cent share of the business. This partner, Spencer Grainger, had been active in the business with the old owner for several years. It seemed to make sense to have someone on board who already knew how things worked. So, Fabian signed the papers, borrowed a few hundred thousand dollars, and bought himself a business. And a partner.

Things turned sour with Spencer in the second year. Fabian started to get creepy emails from the former business owner, where it was clear Spencer had been sharing business information. In fact, it became clear that Spencer was in regular communication with the former owner, undermining Fabian's authority, even handing over proprietary information the old owner no longer had a right to.

Before Fabian knew it, his partner had taken off with both money and clients, rejoining the old owner in their new business. Fabian's business was in a death spiral and he was being summoned to court. Fabian ended up in a protracted legal dispute that took years to settle and cost thousands. It was beyond traumatic. Fabian lost his life savings, the business and a good chunk of his self-esteem. Fabian really couldn't see how things could have turned out any worse.

Time went by, and Fabian eventually started a new business. He thought he had put the bad experience behind him and was truly trying to start fresh. But the experience with Spencer as a business partner left a deep scar. And because he didn't seem to be aware, it was getting in the way of his new business.

Fabian remains fearful that others are out to get him. He's convinced that if he isn't vigilant, he will once again be taken advantage of. He trusts no one and sees nefarious intent where there is none. He believes the worst about people – even those he has known his whole life. The result is that Fabian's relationships are fraught with conflict. Employee relationships, contractor relationships, supplier relationships, you name it. He hires them and fires them, or he hires them and they quit. Fabian can't seem to find people he can trust – because he trusts no one.

Fabian's beliefs are the basis for an attitude focused on the negative outcome he doesn't want. Fabian will attract to his business the only people left that will work with him: the untrustworthy and unethical. He will fall victim to someone again, or he will believe he has fallen victim again, and Fabian will say, "See? I KNEW it. I knew I was going to get screwed."

Belief and Attitude are Choices

Your beliefs and your attitude are the most important factors in your success or failure as an independent professional entrepreneur. Oh, sure, whether you are outgoing or risk averse, full to the brim with new ideas or resilient – these can all make a difference. But they are *personality traits*.

Attitude is a decision. You can decide to see the silvery beauty of the cloud cover or focus on how much you hate the rain. One option will result in better health, better relationships, better life experiences, and better business outcomes. You know the one: sunshine and rainbows.

EuroMaTech delivers about 500 corporate training programs

each year in management, leadership, IT, HR, finance, accounting, and ... the power of attitude.

> *New business requirements, increased performance demands, and a changing workforce mean it is essential for professionals at all levels to understand and master the skills, techniques and methods of positive thinking and positive attitude.*
>
> EuroMaTech

Vince Fowler is a Calgary, Canada-based leadership coach, speaker, and owner of Vested Interest Group. His coaching contracts often begin with a personality quiz, which he explains is simply a self-awareness tool, not a determinant of attitude. The results place his clients into one of four personality quadrants: dominant, inspiring, supportive, or cautious.

> *You can be a successful entrepreneur regardless of which quadrant you're in. It's true more entrepreneurs fall into the dominant quadrant, but that's not what determines their success.*
>
> Vince Fowler, Vested Interest Group

Your birth influences your personality. Your experiences develop your character and fuel your beliefs. It's *awareness* of your beliefs and your *choice* of attitude that will determine your success.

Six Key Principles to Beneficial Attitudes and Beliefs

1. Take ownership of your own shit. You are responsible for your successes, your failures, and everything in between. It is both liberating and a burden to know that you have the power to create your own circumstances, in business and in life.

In Fabian's case, does this mean he was responsible for the traumatic circumstance that led to court appearances and the loss of several thousand dollars? Yes. He isn't responsible for the actions of his former partner or the previous owner, however the decision to enter into the business was his. Every decision as to how to respond to what was happening around him was his. Today, Fabian also owns his perpetual belief that he will get screwed again. Only when he becomes aware enough to own a different belief, attitude, and position, will Fabian truly be free to create a fulfilling and successful business.

2. See past the pain. Entrepreneurial, freelance, or small business endeavours are not for the faint of heart. While it's true there are times of joy and fun, enthusiasm and energy, it is also a rough, dark, and painful journey. Most of the people who quit and go back to working for someone else do so because they don't have the stomach to get past those dark days.

3. Clarity of purpose. When you have clarity of purpose, you will always have the confidence to execute. That means you're willing to put up with lots of discomfort – emotional, financial, sometimes even physical – to do what you know you have to do. Without clarity of purpose, you will not inspire staff, or potential clients, or even suppliers. They will walk. And your business will suffer.

4. Willing to execute. Being an entrepreneur means making decisions and acting without the luxury of having all the facts. Sometimes very few facts. If you're the type of person who prefers not to make your move without knowing all the variables, you'll have a hard time moving your business forward. And moving it forward is the key: go north or go south, it doesn't matter. But standing still will get you nowhere.

5. Embrace failure. Failure is the currency with which success is bought. If you do not fail, you will not learn. If you do not learn, you will not succeed.

Entrepreneurs innovate. Innovation brings problems. If you don't bring the right attitude to the problems you encounter, you'll join the ranks of those who scurry back to their corporate jobs where the perceived risk is lower. Problems and failures contain important messages. Only by embracing them and working through them can you truly benefit from them.

6. Trust your capacity. Trust is such a big issue that it should be it's own book. For now, suffice to say that trusting that you have the capacity to handle anything your business and your life throws at you goes a long way to shedding the fear that traps you in negative beliefs and attitudes. It can bring you significant freedom to pursue your authentic purpose and the business and life of your dreams.

We were between businesses when we threw caution to the wind and went for our big dreams. We'd wrapped up three years of work helping build a young franchise brand. We were about to start the next big project but didn't yet know what that was. We took a look at ourselves, at our ages, at the things we still wanted to do and accomplish, and just went for it. We sold everything. We left friends and family and safety and security and left our beloved Canada. We moved to Mexico, bought a sailboat, and have been living aboard *Ingenium* ever since. We had no guaranteed income, being too young for our pensions to kick in. But we did have trust for our own capacity – both to create the next phase of life as we wanted it and to handle and manage whatever might come next. Some people told us we were crazy, because 'What if?' this or 'What if?' that. Others told us they envied our luck, or circumstance, or whatever external thing they could find to ascribe credit.

The truth is that we trusted – and still do – in our capacity. We take ownership of our own shit, knowing no one else is responsible for our success or failure. We choose to see past the pain of uncertainty, of low-income months when our best clients take a break, to focus on the amazing privilege to live this experience. We have clarity of purpose, in that we know we are creating a life that reflects our desire for geographic independence, authentic living close to the ocean and the outdoors, and a business in Ingenium Books that honours our creative selves and desire to make the world a better place. There is no question we are willing to execute – we did it – and embrace failure in all its forms, whether the possibility or the reality of failure. And we move on to achieve our goals and live our dreams anyway.

Be aware of your beliefs and choice of attitude. Check in and gauge whether they are holding you back or propelling you forward. Remember, the most important factors in your success or failure – as an iPro, freelancer, small business owner or entrepreneur – are your attitude and your beliefs.

3

Panning for Gold

YOUR BUSINESS IDEA

Kelly Niessen always knew she was an entrepreneur. She had the proverbial lemonade stand and other enterprising childhood endeavours. Before she left high school she started looking for her business idea. She worked full-time as she completed her undergrad degree in human resources while looking for her business idea. She held senior executive roles in other businesses, large and small, while looking for her business idea.

As she led telecommunications sales teams, she completed her master's degree in business administration (MBA). Through the case studies and the team work and the advanced mathematics and the site visits, she kept panning for gold, looking for that perfect business idea.

She joined business groups, attended lectures and coffee meetings. She read business journals and magazines and attended business award ceremonies. She volunteered on boards that served the entrepreneurial community. And kept looking for her business idea.

Finally, in 2004, she couldn't wait any longer. She decided to become a business owner by acquisition, instead of inception. She focused on her functional skill set to make sure the business she was buying was going to be a fit with her knowledge, experience and skills.

It wasn't enough. The miss was the culture and the passion. The business she bought – and worked so hard to match with her own carefully analyzed abilities – failed a few years later.

That Elusive Idea

'What am I going to do? What am I good at?' It might take some work to uncover a buried passion or get past the fear of going independent, but what you sell to others will be something you generate directly and personally.

For many would-be entrepreneurs, the thing standing between them and a booming business is an idea. Their personal skill is not necessarily the skill they'll need for that new business. What they want more than anything in the world is to run and grow a business. And it can be difficult to find the right idea.

What product or service? What market? What niche? And, what problem is the idea going to solve? It's the million dollar question, but only half the equation. Don't you also want to align the business idea with your skills, knowledge, passion and character? You might think so. But not always.

As we sat in the audience during a Toronto Franchise Show presentation several years back, franchise expert Gary Prenevost told the crowd that loving the taste of ice cream isn't a good enough reason to start up an ice cream shop. Why not? Because you'll end up spending the bulk of your time managing the part-time work schedules of teenagers, not enjoying North America's second favourite dessert.

Back to Kelly Niessen. She is now co-founder and president of KANDY Outdoor Flooring, a franchised brand that expands home experiences with service, quality, and choice in new outdoor flooring for condo balconies. In the first five years since its inception in 2011, the first-in-class Canadian brand had grown to include franchises in Edmonton, Calgary, North Vancouver, West Vancouver, and Toronto.

How, exactly, did she come up with the idea for KANDY?

> *I didn't come up with my business idea. It came to me. I couldn't find anyone to help spruce up our ugly concrete condo balcony. The thought of turning that into a business literally came to me in the middle of the night.*
>
> Kelly Niessen, Co-founder KANDY Outdoor Flooring

Niessen's story highlights several of the best pieces of advice around generating a solid business idea:

1. It can take dozens of ideas before a winner shows up.
2. The best ideas come from personal experience with a gap in the market.
3. If the idea isn't unique, then the method, process, or result must be better.
4. An idea should align with the founder's passion, culture and interest, rather than his/her functional skill and experience.

> *Creative, game-changing ideas will always have an element of serendipity to them, and will never be producible on demand.*
>
> Robert Tucker, Driving Growth Through Innovation

Serendipity for KANDY co-founders Kelly and Doug happened because they bought that condo and surrounding events triggered the business idea.

Keep dipping your pan into that river silt, shaking it back and forth, and watching for that little gold nugget of a business idea that may show up when you least expect.

> *Don't ask what the world needs. Ask what makes you come alive, and go do it. Because what the world needs is people who have come alive.*
>
> Howard Thurman

4

Why You Dig

BUSINESS PURPOSE

Personal development programs like Tony Robbins, Landmark, or Context International, to name a few, all ask participants to ponder simple questions like, 'Why am I here?', and 'What is really important to me?'. Questions like these are designed to help individuals bring purpose to life.

This approach has an important place in the freelance and small business world, too.

For a long time, we thought of the mission statement as the ultimate strategic direction tool. We've participated in a number of mission statement development sessions held by companies we were either working with, or for. These were often multi-day off-site affairs with an entire leadership team agonizingly wringing out just the right tone to chart a course forward.

Our perspective on mission statements changed when we were working with KANDY Outdoor Flooring. Co-founders Kelly and Doug Niessen had engaged consulting services from Unleash Culture founder David Reeve to help uncover KANDY's purpose – the 'why' the brand exists.

> *Most brands operate in a transactional way of thinking. They focus on what they do and how they do it, but they never address* **why** *they do it.*

David Reeve, Unleash Culture

A clear, concise purpose can give you an edge over your competitors, not for the fact of having a purpose statement, but because customers will care more about you and connect more deeply with you. And, as with the difference between George and Lucy, when you know your purpose, you can also connect more deeply with your customers and potential clients, because your purpose will be about the results you create for people rather than *what you do*.

Your Purpose Statement

So just what is a purpose statement? And how is it different from a mission statement?

- A purpose statement describes both now and forever; a mission statement describes a not-yet-attained future state.
- A purpose statement is the essence of your being; a mission statement is outside of you and apart.
- A purpose statement is a memorable emotional hook while most mission statements are dull and boring.
- A good purpose statement is four words or fewer; most mission statements are too long to remember.

Four words? Yes. Four words are easy to remember, easy to put into action, and create clarity rather than confusion. Most importantly, they generate an emotional response.

Getting a purpose statement that is only four words is not as challenging as you might think, as long as you abandon your old mission statement thinking. Illuminating additional differences between mission and purpose is Reeve's list of what *not* to include in your purpose statement:

- Why your product or service is the best.
- Anything about revenue, cost, or price.
- Anything about what you do or how you do it.
- Anything about quality or your customer service.
- Anything at all about your brand.

Here are a few sample purpose statements that illustrate how they work:

- David Reeve's Unleash Culture: *Discover Greatness Within.*
- Kelly Niessen's KANDY Outdoor Flooring: *Expanding Home Experiences.*
- Our own Ingenium Books: *Breathing Life into Ideas.*
- An IT company: *Creating Peace of Mind.*
- A home care company: *Nurturing the Human Spirit.*

A clear purpose statement that reveals why you exist is especially powerful in today's social media-driven marketing world, where every business, iPro, freelancer and corporation is working to connect individually with customers and clients.

And most paying customers aren't really inspired by things like share value.

> *I have never met an entrepreneur who woke up in the middle of the night, awakened his or her spouse and said, 'Honey, I*

want to start a brand to increase shareholder value through profitability while maintaining environmental standards, blah blah blah.'

David Reeve, Unleash Culture

Be clear about your purpose, hone it to a four-word statement, and broadcast it to the world. Align your prospecting, sales and client service approaches to your purpose statement. And then watch your business or client contracts roll in.

5

Pick Your Mountain

BUSINESS STRUCTURE

Picking the right business structure is like picking which mountain to climb. You can pick one like Everest, suitable for climbing enthusiasts who structure their lives around getting to the top. But not everyone is interested in climbing Everest. It is a complex and expensive endeavour. Once you're on that mountain, there's no quick way down.

Maybe a smaller mountain nearby is the right one for you. You can easily do day hikes and see a new hilltop vista every day. You don't need the expensive gear and you're pretty close to home if anything goes awry. However, you might get to the top and discover it's not quite high enough for what you'd hoped to see.

Effie's Etchings

Effie Berensen has a full-time job with a courier company that she endures but doesn't enjoy. She dreams of being able to leave one day to do her own thing and make her living from her art.

Effie is a talented sketch artist. She can whip out a sheet of drawing paper and her charcoal pencils and within a few minutes capture the likeness of the sparrow on her windowsill, or the iris blooming in the park. She's been giving her sketches away to family and friends for Christmas and birthdays for years.

Now Effie has decided it's time. She finds the forms online for incorporating a business and prints them all. She signs and scans all the documents and sends them electronically to the government. She's sure she'll be ready to give her notice to quit her job soon. Really soon.

Every spare minute Effie now devotes to creating new sketches. Soon she has a respectable pile. She digs into her line of credit and pays for a booth at the local art fair. She sells her first few sketches. (She's ecstatic!) She isn't sure how to accept payment beyond cash and she hasn't figured out how to generate a receipt. She has no idea whether she should be charging tax on top and, if so, how much. She's knows it's time to consult an accountant.

Her accountant gives her some good advice about how to charge tax. He also suggests she's made a mistake by incorporating. It turns out the reality of her business didn't match the legal structure she'd chosen. Effie chose Mount Everest when the hills behind her house would suit her better, financially speaking.

Structure Choices

Where you live and what business activity you're engaged in will dictate the basic requirements for business structure.

Beyond the basics, some choices you make will have lasting impacts on your bottom line. You can choose from a list of structures, including:

- Sole proprietorship (called sole trader in U.K.)
- Partnership
- Corporation

First, let's talk about being a freelancer or iPro.

In Canada and the U.K., you don't need a business licence as long as you're operating under your own legal name. You'll charge and pay the required taxes and you'll include your business activity when you file your personal taxes.

In Australia, on the other hand, if you're doing anything for pay beyond recovering costs, you must get an Australian Business Number, or ABN. Without an ABN you can't register a website. And in the United States if you operate out of your home, you need a Home Occupancy Permit.

Making sure you are clear on the rules for your particular type of freelance business and your jurisdiction is a little like ensuring you know the safe hiking trails. Start with a thorough internet search using a combination of search terms that include what industry you're in, along with the words 'business licence', 'business registration', and your city and country.

If you know you need a business licence and you're all excited to get going on your new business idea, there are two questions you – or your accountant – should ask to determine whether your business should be a sole proprietorship or a corporation.

> *Most people tell me they don't know much about business, the Canada Revenue Agency, or taxes. They're the ones I can help the most. It's the ones who come in first day and announce they've already incorporated that I have to worry about.*
>
> Bill Crysler, Furtney Crysler LLP

To ensure the setup and accounting end of your business makes sense, ask yourself these two questions.

1. Is this your main business?

Many businesses are set up as something on the side, where a full-time job is being maintained to pay the bills and/or keep the contributions to the pension plan going. For example, it's popular right now to make and sell crafts via platforms like Etsy, but it's often not the main gig for the owner. In this case, and others where your business is not your main source of income, sole proprietorship is the way to go.

Here's why: it's simple to set up and register; it's less costly to set up and maintain year over year; and losses can be used to offset personal taxable income.

2. Is your business going to be profitable right away?

We all dream that our businesses will be wildly profitable, but the truth is that isn't always the case. If your business plan projects profit only in years three, four, or five, which is common, perhaps delay incorporation until profitability is imminent and tangible.

Here are some of the advantages of incorporating in Canada (check with a tax professional in your country of residence):

- Income is taxed at the lowest small business tax rate, significantly lower than the personal tax rate that applies with a sole proprietorship.
- Protection from third party creditors.
- Liability protection in most cases (except lenders will still hold you personally responsible for funds you borrow on behalf of your company, and professional corporations such as medical doctors are still held personally liable).
- Tax planning benefits such as tax deferral, control over when you personally receive income, income splitting, and dividend income.

- Your business name is protected throughout the jurisdiction in which you incorporate, whether provincially or federally.

There's also the cost of incorporating and the annual filing requirements.

The one-time cost of incorporation, in Canada at least, will run you $1500 - $3000, and the ongoing fees for your financial statements and corporate tax return could be another $2500 every year.

In addition to increased cost, there are other disadvantages to incorporation to be aware of:

- Paperwork! Corporate documents such as bylaws and minutes, the register of directors, share register, and the transfer register must all be kept current.
- In addition to your personal tax return, you have to file a separate tax return for the corporation each year.
- No personal tax credits for your corporation. Every new dollar earned is taxed.
- It's difficult and costly to wind up a corporation should you decide to close down your business.

Effie knows now that before she picked her mountain and decided on a legal business structure, she should have consulted a lawyer, a bookkeeper, and an accountant.

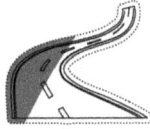

6

Yellow Brick Road

THE BUSINESS PLAN

There are certain types of people we'll call 'Fly By Your Seat Pete' or 'Who Needs a Plan Stan'. Pete and Stan for short. These loveable wind-flutterers tend to be great idea generators and poor finishers. They don't know there's a yellow brick road or that following it will lead to bigger, better, finer things.

Without squashing the creativity in our beloved Pete, or if you think this sounds like you, we're going to give you a little advice. (Stan, sit back down.) If you're planning to embark on professional activities to earn money, it will pay off to plan ahead. Even for you, Pete.

Whether you're an iPro or you design websites from your sofa, putting together a bit of a plan makes sense. Oh, yes, we are talking about your business plan.

Your business plan is a foundational document. It might be a short and sweet few pages, or your business may be more involved and complex requiring a three-to-five year cash flow projection. Either way, the basic principles and elements of a good business plan are the same.

Whether you're testing the waters on your business idea, looking for funding, or attracting equity investors, the quality of your business plan – and the soundness of your financials – is key.

Pete and Stan would sign the office lease and sales deals before working through the financials. Bad idea.

> *You have to have a good handle on the financials if you want to move forward confidently. People usually underestimate how much money they need to start a business. When we write their plan and start going through the numbers, we often discover its three times their original guess.*
>
> Arlene Anderson, BusinessAdvice.com

Your business plan will help you see clearly how much business you need to pull in to pay the mortgage and feed the kids. It will give you a focus for your daily, weekly and monthly activities. And it will help you identify the buyers of your products or services.

Business Plan Outline

With the preceding tips in mind, use this outline as a guide for writing your business plan.

1. **Executive Summary**
2. Highlights
3. Objectives of the business
4. Vision/mission/purpose/values
5. **Business Description**
6. Ownership and legal structure
7. Location and hours (might be global and 24/7)
8. Products and services
9. Suppliers

10. Manufacturing
11. General management, and financial management
12. Summary of startup activities
13. **Marketing**
14. Market analysis
15. Segmentation
16. Competition
17. Pricing
18. **Financial**
19. Startup expenses and capital requirements
20. Cash flow forecast (36 months)
21. Income projection
22. Profit and loss statement, balance sheet
23. Sales forecast
24. Break-even analysis.

Whether you write your own business plan or hire expert help, the finished product should reflect the following ten qualities.

1. Behaves Like a Roadmap

Your business plan should include all the milestones, targets and steps you'll need to take as your business moves through its startup and growth phases.

2. Acknowledges Risk

The number of business owners whose plans claim there's no risk is equal to the number of businesses that live in a fantasy world. And then fail. No business venture is without risk, and your potential investors, supporters and partners know it.

3. Acknowledges Competition

Every successful business has competitors. Some are direct competitors, doing or selling the same thing as you. Others are indirect competitors, on the periphery of the space in which you're planning to be, but still an option for potential customers. Even if you're the first mover, you'll be revealing the market space that – so far – no one else has tapped. All you've got is a head start.

4. Well Written

Grammatical and spelling mistakes won't engender confidence. Aim for a writing style that investors and supporters will enthusiastically want to support: confident, authoritative, and formal. Avoid writing in a style that is too casual, arrogant, or sloppy.

5. Presentation Counts

Your confident and authoritative writing style won't be recognized if your spacing is off, your headings inconsistent, your graphics elementary, and page numbers are missing or incomplete. Sell your great content with flawless presentation.

6. Complete

Your plan should answer all the questions your reader may have. Keep proprietary or highly confidential material out of the executive summary. Place it in an appendix that you can share once you gauge the interest and intent of your prospective partner. Request that they sign a non-disclosure agreement (NDA) before you share.

7. ...But Not Too Complete

Don't let the technical facts or language get in the way of a clear story. Technical specifications, drawings, and data can be included in an appendix.

8. Reasonable Assumptions

Every new business starts out with more assumptions than data. Purchasing behaviour, market demand, and commercialization time are examples. Reasonable assumptions can be supported by checking and citing industry standards and credible research. Don't bury your assumptions in a list of facts.

9. Research

Every assumption about your market, products, services, pricing, and financial projections should be reached after careful research. You should know everything about every competitor, including their size and market share.

10. Solid Financials

Startup expenses, supplies, location, equipment, marketing and advertising, legal and insurance, and administration costs should all be represented in detail with a projection out three to five years. Too quick a path to profitability will stand out as a red flag.

It's okay to complete a business plan only to discover the initiative isn't as grand as you thought. You're simply on a different yellow brick road than you anticipated at the beginning of your journey.

7

Online Cornerstones

CHOOSING THE RIGHT WEB TEAM

When it comes to creating your online presence, choosing the right team to work with you on building your website and often your social profile is a cornerstone of your approach. The wrong team = the wrong results.

Kelly Niessen, introduced earlier, was preparing to launch her brand into the U.S., where she needed a different web presence. She rebuilt her Canadian site four times in the first five years of operation, partly to address the maturing brand and its purpose, and partly to address evolving technical needs like bandwidth and hosting limitations.

The Canadian site of KANDY Outdoor Flooring focused on the *Service, Quality, Choice* value proposition delivered by franchise partners present in major centres across Canada. KANDY's proprietary outdoor flooring products were not generally available for purchase online.

KANDY Outdoor Flooring in the U.S. was to be mainly an online store where customers could choose and order their product for self-installation. The *Service, Quality, Choice* value proposition was still valid, but with a decidedly online and telephone support model.

She had hired and worked with several different web development teams based in Canada. For the U.S. e-commerce site she selected a company based in Spain.

> "A project that was supposed to take eight weeks wasn't finished in five months. I fired the firm and lost a chunk of money on the project.
>
> Kelly Niessen, KANDY Outdoor Flooring

Building a website takes time, care, attention, and money. There are some common problems with website projects:

- the strategy doesn't align with the results
- the content doesn't match the personality of the brand
- it doesn't attract enough of the right leads, or
- the site isn't ready for launch.

> It took me over a year to get a website up, which is ridiculous. I'm not convinced that the web world actually knows what it's doing at all, and I've had more than one experience with one person.
>
> Lynn Williams, The Lifestyle Protector

When these problems arise, it's expensive, labour intensive, and can be devastating to a small business. Unless you're in the business of developing websites, you should hire a professional.

But which professional? That's where it gets tricky. There are often legal requirements that a finished website product must meet, usually relating to protection of privacy and the collection and storage of private email addresses. Remember, in Australia you need a business number before you can get a website. However, the people who develop and build those websites are not regulated or organized into any kind of association – at least not in Canada.

So what do you do? How do you know? First you need the right team to get your website happening. Here are five things to ask before you hire a web design team.

1. What is your technical approach? It's a complex interplay of concepts: from technical to design, from functionality to behavioural analysis, from the first wire frame to platform and page creation. Then there are the linkages, the search engine optimization (SEO), user experience, and the conversion funnel. Listen to the responses to your question and be sure it ticks all the boxes on your web strategy.

2. How will you translate my brand personality into the copy? You are looking for a writer who wants to read everything you've written about your business: your business plan, your marketing strategy, your brand guide, your customer personas. If you haven't developed these yet, you want a writer who wants to interview you in detail about your market, your customers, your strategy, your differentiators, and not just about your products and services.

3. What's your view on image selection? You are looking for responses that indicate the team you're considering understands the importance and the power of imagery and the role images play in reinforcing your strategy and your message. Picking pretty pictures that don't relate to your brand purpose or your clientele will not engage your visitors and will not help you convert leads into customers.

4. How will you respect my brand's visual identity? You've probably worked hard picking the right colours and design elements for your brand. You want someone working on your web content who will exactly match your logo colours and respect them in the design throughout the site.

5. Can you fill all the key roles? As entrepreneurs, especially when starting out, it's natural to do a piecemeal approach so you only spend money when you absolutely need to. Hire someone to manage your Google Adwords. Then someone else to do SEO on your site. Someone else to add new pages, change the layout. You get the idea. Unfortunately, this can cause more problems than it solves.

Consider your website a cornerstone of all your business activity. Don't lose sight of the big picture, which is how seamlessly and how well your website represents you, your business, and your brand.

8

Terra Firma

THE LEGAL BASICS

S tarting, running, and growing a small business, even a freelance one, involves a lot of 'bootstrapping': digging into your own resources, financial and otherwise, to get things done. In order to keep your feet firmly and safely planted on terra firma, there are legal matters you want to address with a professional. And yes, we do mean a lawyer.

Sign of the Times

Casey Adler had been planning the grand opening of his new guitar shop for months. He'd found the perfect location, close to the big Long and McQuade mega-music outlet where the musically inclined already shopped for everything from amps and woodwind reeds to MIDI cables and mixing boards.

Adler's custom-made guitar shop (and repair shop in the back) is for the serious aficionado who knows exactly what they want in their instrument and can't find in a mass-produced Martin or Fender.

Adler paid the first six months of the lease up front. From the first time he saw the storefront retail space, he was in love. He loved its plate-glass feature window and aging wood-framed front door; the brass bell that tinkled with every open and close; the century-old maple floorboards that sprayed glittering dust particles like silver confetti with each step. And the smell! Like old books and metal, with a hint of lubricating oil from some long-ago endeavour.

The day before his planned grand opening, Casey dragged his ladder onto the sidewalk out front. He measured and drilled the holes for the heavy duty screws to hold up the sign that would hang perpendicular to the façade out over the sidewalk. It was an artisan wrought iron frame, with leaf-ended curlicues, three feet long and 18 inches high. Hung from heavy black links at the bottom of the frame was a hand-crafted, carved, scorched and shellacked maple wood sign: *Adler Acoustics*.

"Excuse me, are you Casey Adler?" Adler turned carefully from the second-from-the-top ladder rung to see a bespectacled man, rumpled and in his mid-forties, carrying a clipboard. Casey thought, "A bylaw inspector, already?"

Casey had to remove his precious sign immediately. City by-laws prohibited any storefront signs from protruding out from the façade further than 24 inches. No exceptions, the decision was final. His perfectly planned grand opening would be happening without his beloved sign!

Checking it Twice

The mistake Casey Adler made was in not consulting his lawyer before he signed the lease, or at least before he spent the money on his sign. A good lawyer would have checked the relevant bylaws for the neighbourhood and provided advice for things like signage, parking, and more. The $2500 he'd just spent on that beautiful sign was wasted.

Even in today's online world, many businesses require physical space: office space, retail space, storefront, or otherwise. If you do not have an ongoing relationship with a lawyer when you are ready to sign that lease, you may be making one of your most expensive mistakes. Say you're considering a lease for $2K per month. That's $120K over five years! Without a legal review before you sign that lease you don't know what you're getting into.

The amount you will spend upfront by consulting a lawyer is a relatively small price to pay to be well prepared for a business grand opening like Casey's.

Signage clauses are often problem areas. Landlords and tenants often disagree about what constitutes 'appropriate' signage, and a lawyer-reviewed lease document before you sign could save you bundles down the road.

Insurance

Insurance is another area where the bootstrapping entrepreneur is often tempted to cut corners. Here's a question: if you can't afford insurance, can you afford to be in business?

The right insurance coverage is actually a prudent investment should you need to make a claim. Here are the most commonly avoided types of insurance.

Auto

Any business use of a vehicle should be carefully scrutinized against the insurance rules in your jurisdiction. Auto insurance is mandatory in Canada and provincially regulated, so exactly how your premiums and policy apply to how you use your vehicle will differ depending on where you live. In the United States, auto insurance is mandatory in all states, except New Hampshire, which requires that you be financially responsible. In the U.K. and Australia, you must have third party liability insurance at a minimum. In 2017, the E.U. determined that there should be a common system of guaranteed coverage, even if a driver is uninsured. You get the point: check the rules in your jurisdiction.

Tools

It's common for tradesmen to accumulate tens of thousands of dollars' worth of expensive tools. If they aren't properly insured, the investment isn't protected.

Health and 'Key Man' Insurance

These policies help protect the business and any partners in the event that key personnel become ill or pass away.

Power of Attorney

Power of attorney is not just for the mentally infirm. A general power of attorney (POA) can give your lawyer, for example, authority to manage all or part of your property and finances as long as you are mentally capable of managing your affairs. The general POA terminates if you do become mentally incapacitated. The advantage would be realized in the case of a business owner engaged in frequent travel, like those of us who are digital nomads: no need to fly back home to sign important documents before a deadline – your lawyer can do it for you under a general POA.

Partnership Agreements

Partnerships of one form or another are common, including spouses that decide to go into business together. You're not alone if you consider partnership and shareholder agreements to be an unnecessary expense. But you would be wrong.

> *Without partnership agreements there are often arguments, especially over liabilities accrued while in operation, as to how to wind up the business, which leads to litigation.*

Valentine Lovekin, Lovekin Law

What About Those Free Templates?

Using free online templates, writing DIY agreements, or skimping on insurance policies may save you a few dollars at the front end. But it could end up costing you dearly when you need help the most.

Because every business has its own unique elements, its own unique needs, and its own unique legal requirements, relying on a template is a little like buying a lottery ticket. You just don't know what you're getting. You have no idea whether the off-the-shelf agreement will actually protect your business if you should ever need to defend yourself or assert your rights in court. And that's the whole purpose of a legal agreement.

As a freelancer, you may not have need of every one of these agreements. But being an iPro or entrepreneur is all about being innovative and taking risks – with an eye on upside market success.

Cutting corners on insurance and legal agreements is a risk that could turn your terra firma into quicksand in the time it takes to call your lawyer.

9

Rock Solid

INTELLECTUAL PROPERTY PROTECTION

W e live in a global knowledge economy, and there's a better-than-good chance your business uses at least some knowledge as its currency. Which means it's important to ensure you have a rock solid understanding of intellectual property.

Intellectual property, or IP, is often underestimated or misunderstood. IP is 'creation of the mind' and includes patents, copyrights, trademarks, industrial design, and trade secrets. It can also include your terms of service and non-disclosure and non-compete agreements. Every business is based on an idea, from ground-breaking research that leads to a new drug or technology or product, to new ways of applying good ideas that have come before.

Ideas, Ideas

John, co-author of this book, is an idea guy. He's always thinking about how things can be done better, how processes or tools can be improved, how he can make things more efficient and effective.

Before we moved onto our sailboat to cruise the Pacific coast of

Mexico, we were avid summer campers. We loved to camp, taking our big tent and small backpacks into Algonquin or Killarney Provincial Parks, where we picked out just the right spot far away from visible neighbours. We loved the quiet, the woodsy scents, the required self-sufficiency. It was during one such trip in about 2010 that John had a idea for a way to make one of the activities we repeat over and over again easier and more efficient. And he would ultimately develop it into a patent-pending product.

We can't tell you much about the product itself because, at the time of this writing, we are in licensing negotiations with a firm that may end up manufacturing and selling John's invention. But it does make the outdoor living experience more enjoyable, particularly when it comes to lighting and maintaining a campfire. John developed a makeshift prototype that we used over several camping seasons. We conducted our own market research, walking through and checking every other campsite for any sign of a similar product. We searched all the outdoor recreation stores we could find and of course we searched online. We found nothing at all like John's invention.

We know from personal experience how exciting it is to come up with something that appears to be a market first, and how tempting it is to shout it from the rooftops and tell family, friends and colleagues. And we know how important it is to understand what you're dealing with and to be circumspect until the time is right.

> *A lot of people end up stepping on their own toes by speaking about their ideas too early. They don't file a provisional patent application because they haven't done their research or spoken to the right professionals.*
>
> Dr. Gabriella Chan, Yocto Law

Provisional Patents

In our case, we hired a patent agent – after getting him to sign a non-disclosure agreement – to do a rigorous search for any similar patents, granted or pending, and for prior art. Prior art, in patent law, is any sign whatsoever that your invention has been conceived, discussed, or shared by someone else. It doesn't have to be commercially for sale and it doesn't even have to physically exist. It just needs to have been described or drawn by someone else and be the same or very close to your invention.

Once that search had concluded, confirming there was nothing similar and no prior art, we proceeded to our patent application.

It took several weeks to complete all specifications, technical drawings, and descriptions of use. We filed the application and received our confirmation documents from the relevant patent offices, finally ready to take the next step, which was to research and carefully approach companies we thought might be interested in licensing our patented product idea and running with it.

The Risk of Low-Cost

Robert Irani is an intellectual property lawyer as well as a U.S. patent attorney, U.S. trademark attorney, and Canadian patent agent. He says the cost of properly preparing a patent application, in particular, can be prohibitive to many small business owners. However, trying to save money with so-called cookie-cutter templates will cost you more in the long run.

> *You may save a few bucks on the front end, but you get a patent application that isn't very good. Later you may discover a problematic piece of prior art, for example, and your patent, and potentially your business, gets knocked out of the water.*

Robert Irani, Patent Attorney/Patent Agent

Many companies will employ a number of IP streams as they grow and evolve. How you employ them, and when, will be dictated by your business strategy.

Six tips for your business IP

1. Inform yourself about IP. Do your homework about IP and what it means for your business. Take advantage of the free, easily-accessible resources available through the Canadian Intellectual Property Office, the United States Patent and Trademark Office, or the World Intellectual Property Organization. If you're an iPro, be sure your client contracts specify who retains the rights to the IP.

2. Pursue provisional patents early. Be excited about your idea, of course, and be ultra-cautious about with whom and how you share information. If you're unsure, consult with a licensed patent agent or patent attorney. You cannot publish information about your idea on your website or start to sell or market it in any way if you hope to obtain a patent.

3. Ask for help from the right people. Go with the pros. Resist the temptation to save money by handling protection of your IP on your own. That is short-term thinking that could cost you everything in the long run.

4. Realistically consider geography. Patents and trademarks filed in Canada, for example, will protect you only in Canada. On the other hand, there's no need to go through the time and expense of filing and registering globally if your realistic market will remain in North America.

5. Ensure there is a market. Technically this is general business advice, not just IP. Gabriella Chan, quoted earlier in this chapter, says that nine out of every ten businesses fail in the first five years because they've created "fantastic solutions for non-existent problems".

6. Pursue production options. How will your patent-pending idea get to market? If it is a physical product, what materials will be used and what do they cost? Does your product require specially-sized manufacturing equipment that will drive production costs up? If it is a knowledge-based patent idea, who do you need to employ or engage in order to bring your idea to market and how much will this cost?

If we were starting our patent pursuit over again, step number six is one we'd tackle earlier, before reaching out to potential licensees or buyers. We discovered that design modifications were required in order to get manufacturing costs into a reasonable range for competitive consumer pricing.

You want your understanding of IP to be rock solid, but your actual IP strategy to be flexible. Because your IP strategy falls under your business strategy, not the other way around, business objectives and market factors may mean your IP strategy needs to shift.

Regardless, understand where you may have intellectual property in your business and be sure you set out to protect it.

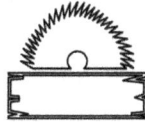

10

Nose to the Grindstone

SYSTEMS & PROCESS

Y ou may have started your business with an incredible idea, some initiative, creativity, and maybe even a bit of cash. Did you also think about the need for systems: the procedures, principles and processes that both describe and dictate how you and your business actually get things done? If not, you'll keep your nose to the grindstone and work a lot harder than you have to.

Spotting the Problem

Dara Sklar had been working for 11 years as an operations manager in her father's company. Life was good. She married her best friend Shane and they'd saved up the money for a down payment in the hopping real estate market that was Vancouver, Canada.

The realtor they worked with, Remus Venture, was always dressed in suit and tie and his business card was well designed and glossy. While checking for properties online, Dara decided to check out the website listed on the back of Venture's business card.

She got a 404 error. She typed in the URL once, twice, then a third time. Nope. Nothing. She called him up right away.

"Remus! There's a problem with your website," Dara told him, her index finger clicking to see if a refresh would bring the site up. "You're handing out business cards with a web address that doesn't work!"

Venture confided that he was not good with administration or managing his own website. Dara offered to help. She got his website functioning and set up systems for him to manage his bills and his books.

Before she knew it, Dara had a handful of realtor clients she was helping in the same way. Then a dozen, then 40. She was helping others set up systems, but she didn't yet have any systems for her own business as a virtual assistant (VA). And then she needed to hire her own VA.

> My mistake was not putting processes and systems in place before I got really busy. Only when I was forced did I create a process for someone not in the same room with me.
>
> Dara Sklar, Synced With Dara

The Freedom of Process

Sklar found a sense of freedom she hadn't yet experienced in her business. Later, when she had to replace that first assistant, everything was ready for the next. This experience was so profound that she's translated it into her next business venture: Synced With Dara has a mission to help other entrepreneurs organize and digitize paperwork and files.

Freeing up time and energy for the business founder is a significant benefit to systematizing business processes. It is also the key to sustainable business growth.

> *Getting to a level that satisfies your growth plan does not come just by hiring some people, building a product or giving a service. You really need to start thinking about systems early on.*

Farid Dordar, PerfectMind

Like Sklar, it was Farid Dordar's experience from his first business that led him to the second. PerfectMind offers a software product that allows you to customize your business processes. Every business, even within the same industry, has different system needs because every owner will run his/her business differently. Every business can consider systems in every area.

Sales and marketing

- Prospecting, telemarketing, and direct mail.
- Analysis of sales and product performance.
- Trends and marketing channels.
- Sales order processes.
- Customer acquisition and retention.

Human resources

- Recruiting and interviewing processes.
- Compensation and bonus metrics.
- Payroll and tracking of employee hours.

Finance and accounting

- Align objectives throughout the organization.
- Business-wide visibility on key performance indicators.

- Inventory control and analysis.
- Supplier relationships and interactions.
- Profitability analysis.

Putting in the time and effort to document, implement, and analyze processes results in fewer headaches and less stress, while increasing satisfaction and upside business results.

You're already keeping your nose to the grindstone starting and running your small business. Why work harder than you have to?

STEP II

Mine Your Quarry

11

Beware Fools' Gold

CONQUER CASH FLOW

H er stomach fell to the floor, doing a loop-de-loop all the way down. The customer on the other end of the line – the fourth this week – complained of a faulty product and was asking for a fix or a refund. Or both.

Gillian asked the questions she already knew the answer to, wrote down the details she had already memorized, and promised a resolution she knew would put the business further into the red. The margins for this new product had been set without consideration for the kinds of problems that were arising now. The income from that sale had already been spent on ordering the next batch of product – which was also likely faulty and couldn't be sold.

Gillian and Steve had sunk everything they had into this business. They'd quit their corporate jobs. They invested much of their retirement savings and started their own new painting and decor business.

Their business provided and applied self-cleaning indoor-outdoor waterproof paint. No more washing walls! A new development in paint technology involved inserting titanium dioxide nanoparticles. After application, any moisture or water droplets would slide down the paint surface, washing dirt, bacteria and viruses away.

Gillian and Steve had a licensing agreement with the patent holders and their business plan was impressive. Their enthusiasm fuelled a classic entrepreneurial mistake. They believed so much in their projection numbers that they forgot they were just *projections*, not fact. Their previous corporate and business experience didn't protect them from poor cash flow management, and this compounded the problem. They overspent on marketing and under-estimated the reserves they'd need in case something unexpected came along.

And then the product started failing – in large applications in commercial locations (read, big sales) and small indoor-outdoor residential settings. Every sale from a particular batch of paint product was not, apparently, waterproof. The water droplets would roll down the surface alright, but it would take colour with it. The colour would puddle, and when it dried it left crusty little coloured spots. In one costly case, a wealthy client's original oil painting hung on one wall was ruined. It was Tom Thomson's 'Forest Branches' painting, and they'd only recently acquired it from a fine art auction house for over $100,000.

If the painting had been framed traditionally, the canvas would never have come in contact with the wall. But they had wanted something a little more contemporary, so they'd re-framed it in a canvas wrap-style over ¾-inch wood – where Thomson's canvas came into direct contact with the wall. A wall that was supposed to be protected from moisture and rainfall by an awning, but wasn't. And the new paint that was supposed to be waterproof, wasn't.

The client's insurance might have covered the damage, but when insurance adjusters visited the site in the process of assessing the claim, it was clear the problem was faulty paint product. So, no coverage.

The value of that painting was a third of one year's total sales for Gillian and Steve. They didn't have the funds to compensate their client and their general business insurance didn't cover this type of product failure. Countering the reputation damage from the social media campaign the upset clients undertook was futile. Impossible.

In just three years, Gillian and Steve went from feeling like a million bucks and on top of the world launching a new business to personally bankrupt. Their story is a fairly common one: born of optimism, killed by the reality of poor cash flow management.

Cash Flow Really is King

Your hard work, great ideas, solid customer base, and popular products or services are nothing if you can't effectively manage your cash flow. It's one of the biggest challenges for any entrepreneur.

Treating money that comes in like it's a windfall and over-spending turns it into fools' gold. With you as the fool.

Waiting for money to come in can lead to a serious cash flow crunch even for a profitable, growing company. Running out of cash forces a surprising number of otherwise profitable companies to go out of business.

Cash flow management isn't going to fix fundamental flaws, but it's a critical tool in your toolkit. Here are five key steps to master your business cash flow and thrive.

1. Project Cash Flow

Your cash flow projections, plotted on a yearly calendar, will let you spot the peaks and valleys and give you time to create a plan to hang on to some of the revenue from the peaks to cover your expenses in the valleys. (The best tool we've found for this is in Quicken, but only the PC version. Since we switched lock, stock, and barrel for Mac computers – and phones and everything else – we haven't yet found a comparable alternative.) Projections also give you the flexibility to play with scenarios and options. This can be a valuable decision-making tool when it shows you it's not the right time to make an investment in technology or order another container-load of product from overseas.

2. Track Receivables, Expenses & Inventory

Your cash flow projection provides the baseline data that allows you to compare how you're actually doing with how you expected to do. You might wish to do this check-in monthly or weekly. And it's a good idea to use your actual data to update your projections once every quarter.

The metrics you'll want to track include how long it takes your customers to pay you (your average collection period), how long it takes you to pay your bills, your cash on hand, how many days it takes you to sell your inventory, and your inventory turnover.

3. Finance When You Can

Treat your cash flow as king, especially when it comes time to purchase that new vehicle, rebuild your website, or expand your product line. That means don't use your cash when financing will do nicely. Lenders are more likely to extend financing to something tangible than they are when you come in, hat in hand, looking for help because you blew through your cash and then hit an unexpected slump.

Worried about overdoing it on loans? Be sure to tie the term of the loan to the lifespan of the asset you're borrowing against. If you expect the new truck to last five years, don't take on a loan with a seven-year amortization period.

4. Get Paid Faster

One of those numbers you're tracking in step number two – your average collection period – will tell you if there's room to make changes to help your customers pay you faster. Look at your own processes and ensure you're issuing invoices as quickly as possible. And by all means use technology! Don't send your invoices by snail mail when email delivers almost instantly! Make it easy for customers to pay electronically, either via a secure web portal or through mobile payment options that your field staff can whip out to collect while they're on the customer premises. Consider offering discounts for quick payment and charging late fees for customers who take their time. Or require payment up front, in full.

5. Control Outflows of Cash

By all means, pay your bills on time. But there's no reason to pay them before you need to. If you have bills with net 30-day payment terms, pay on day 29 or 30, not on day two. Keep the extra cash working for you for those additional 27 days. Consider leveraging credit cards, too. Pay the bill by credit card when it's due and then pay the balance off the credit card in another 30 days before the interest charges kick in. And, of course, keep a close eye on expenditures and watch for opportunities to reduce.

It's not magic, but poor cash flow management can be, and has been, the downfall of many profitable businesses, big and small. Resist the fools' gold approach. Get a handle on cash flow and keep your stomach - and your business - from loop-de-looping to the floor.

12

Culture Rocks

BUILDING A GREAT BUSINESS CULTURE

C ulture rocks in one of two ways: it can be a rockin' good culture that propels you to higher profits and all round satisfaction, or it can be the rocks just below the surface that put a big hole in your hull. Then you sink.

Culture in Action

Jackson Manonell arrived for his first day of training at Starbucks, ready and excited to begin his new job as a barista.

He was escorted through the wood-panelled coffee shop, past the glass pastry displays and the barista station with its copper coffee machines, then around the counter into the back of the store. Suddenly the slick cleanliness of the customer area turned to functional storage. Shelves were stacked floor to ceiling with boxes of coffee cups, labelled Tall 8oz, Grande 16oz, and Venti 20oz. Large silver bags of coffee beans, racks of fresh croissants, brownies, and cookies. Black tubs filled with individual sugar packets, forks, spoons and knives, small foil pouches of dried berries and green matcha tea.

The manager sat at a solitary desk piled high with papers, markers, and empty beverage cups. A half-eaten breakfast sandwich lay forgotten on a plate. An older model HP laptop was open in front of her and her hands were poised over the keyboard.

"Welcome to Starbucks," Nubia Debrett exclaimed, standing up and opening her arms wide. "It's so nice to have you on the team!"

Nubia accompanied Jackson down the back stairwell into the basement, where more beverage cup boxes and other Starbucks products sat waiting to be stocked on the customer-facing shelves upstairs. There was also a row of round tables and chairs along one wall where staff could sit in peace on their breaks. It was at one of these tables that Nubia dropped her stack of binders and motioned to Jackson to take a seat.

Training a new barista at Starbucks takes a full three days. You might be thinking, "How long does it take to train someone to make coffee?" Ah, but that's the difference. Baristas at Starbucks do much more than make and serve coffee. They deliver an *experience* to everyone that walks in the door.

Jackson learned that Starbucks strives to be the 'third place' for its customer. There's home, there's work… and there's Starbucks. That third place where you always feel comfortable, where you walk in and people smile and know your name. Jackson's training of course included learning about the different types of coffee: the aromas, the intricate flavour differences between a robust bold with a berry aftertaste, or the mild roast and its hint of citrus. He learned the pairings of coffees with types of food and he learned how to measure and make a latte, a frappuccino, and a straight up espresso shot.

Much of his training, however, focused on how Jackson was to create that 'third place' experience for the customer. Look them in the eye and smile. Learn and remember their name, and their drink. Ask them how their day is going. Notice when they first open the door and walk in – and wave to them. Chat up the customers waiting for their drinks to be made. Let them know where their drink is in the line. (*"I've got a grande decaf soy Americano misto for Boni, up next!"*) Jackson also had to learn the Starbucks mission statement:

> *To inspire and nurture the human spirit – one person, one cup and one neighbourhood at a time.*

> Starbucks mission statement

This is the Starbucks culture in action. It is undoubtedly responsible for the success of the international chain and its 25,734 stores around the world.

You're Never Too Small

If you think culture doesn't matter for you, because you're an iPro or your business is too small, we've got news.

Culture is your values put into practice, and it is ultimately about people and relationships. Who do you do business with? People. Culture relates to everything human in your business – how you treat people, your clients, and your employees. It's how you behave. In short, your business culture is your business character.

In his 2016 book *Unleash Culture: How to Design, Implement and Sustain a Powerful Culture that Accelerates the Growth of Your Brand*, David Reeve describes character as the magnet that emotionally attracts people to engage your services.

What kind of culture you create says a lot about you and your business. And it gives people both inside and outside your business a lot to say, too. Doesn't it make sense to try to ensure they're saying good things?

The best opportunity you have to create a winning culture in your business is at the beginning. It's easy to overlook or ignore culture when you're in the startup phase, because there's just so much other stuff to worry about. On top of that, creating culture is not easy, by any stretch. It's complex, it's often misunderstood, and it's easy to get it wrong.

Businesses either *design* their cultures or let them manifest, as Reeve says, *by default.*

Invasive Weeds

Once negative culture takes root, it is like an invasive weed in your garden. Pulling it up by its roots will not eradicate it. It takes a complete overhaul of the garden – remove and destroy all plants, rework the soil to infuse new nutrients, plan the layout of the new garden, and slowly add new healthy plants.

> *The best approach is to try a concept on for size, see how it fits, make changes where necessary and then when it starts to feel just right, introduce another concept and so on. It can take years to implement everything. But the incremental gains you will achieve will culminate in a significant culture shift.*
>
> David Reeve, Unleash Culture

Five culture killers:

1. Always being late to meetings. It shows you don't respect other's time.
2. Not bothering to set up systems that help you or your people do their work.

3. Blaming staff, or clients, or customers, or partners – anybody except yourself and the leadership team – for problems with culture.
4. Spending more time and energy recruiting and hiring than on motivating and inspiring current team members.
5. Limiting participation in brand goal-setting exercises to the top leadership.

Five ways to start building a great culture:

1. Be clear about your purpose, preferably in four words or less, and articulate your top four core values. Align all decisions with these.
2. Engage across and through the brand for strategic planning to build internal brand ambassadors. If you're an iPro, engage key stakeholders and clients.
3. Adopt trust and transparency: share all relevant business metrics (revenue, gross margins, performance metrics, gross profit, client retention, staff retention, etcetera) with everyone associated with the brand.
4. Practice gratitude, optimism and humility. Pay attention to the emotional energy of your brand and, as leader, be accountable for setting the tone.
5. Incorporate character – not just skill – into your brand's story. You can have a story without being clear on your culture, but you can't have a strong culture without being clear on your story.

Culture reflects the character of your brand and the character of your people. Character is responsible for the emotional hook that can cultivate a fan club and create raving brand ambassadors.

Connect your vision to the culture you need in order to realize it. Leverage your unique rockin' good culture to satisfaction and success. And remember:

66 *Culture eats strategy for breakfast.*

Peter Drucker

13

Pinnacle Client Service
TRUST, CREATING VALUE, AND RESULTS

Ensuring you deliver rock solid client service is key to your future, regardless of your business size or structure. If you aren't delivering customer or client service to the pinnacle of your potential today, you're not likely long for this world. In virtually all sectors, competition is fierce and customers can search and switch to the other guy at the drop of a hat.

The team at GoDaddy, the world's leading domain registrar, would win our Pinnacle Service Awards, if we had them. Their 24/7 customer service is already award winning and, in our experience, they deserve every accolade.

The GoDaddy Experience

Under our former 2GreatGuys Inc. umbrella, we had functioning websites for our two existing business niches. One was 2greatguys.com, where John showcases his inventions and directs potential licensing partners to a secure password-protected page. The other was bclearwriting.com, which Boni uses for her writing services and author website. We needed a third to be the platform for Ingenium Books, our self-publishing support service for authors. John had GoDaddy secure the domain (ingeniumbooks.com) and enable Wordpress hosting. Then he went to work building the new site.

A Roadblock

The blue-green glow of John's computer screen in the dark lit up his face like a haunted house cartoon character. He hadn't said a word for several hours, dragging and dropping, writing new lines of code, learning the benefits and limitations of the new theme we'd chosen from Thrive Themes. Then he hit a roadblock.

It didn't matter that it was after midnight. John opened Skype on his laptop and keyed in the number to GoDaddy's 24/7 support line. The recorded voice was friendly, informative, and easy. John chose 'technical support' from the list of service options provided by the recorded voice, and was told his wait would be two minutes.

He actually waited about a minute and a half. (Under-promise, over-deliver!) The GoDaddy agent was knowledgeable, friendly, and solved John's problem. He pointed out a way we could save some money on other items in our account. A pleasant and satisfying experience, all in under 20 minutes.

The agent closed the call by alerting John to a survey that would be arriving shortly by email, explaining that John's responses would be directly linked to this agent's performance.

Surveys help you keep on top of how your customers experience your service. Linking them to the person actually delivering the service to the customer is brilliant.

Our GoDaddy example is fairly simplistic. Creating, analyzing, and improving customer experience, especially in larger small businesses, can be rather complex.

Customer-centric Complexity

Toronto-based Prompta Consulting Group specializes in helping companies that aim to become more customer-centric. This kind of culture transformation takes time and won't succeed unless it has the full engagement of leadership at the top.

> *It needs to work its way all the way through the entire organization. It needs to be tied to the direction of the company, how people are going to be rewarded, how they're measured, and it needs to be tied to processes and procedures.*
>
> Tim Morton, Prompta Consulting Group

Prompta's job is to get people thinking and working in different ways in order to truly become customer focused. And while Canadian Prompta tends to work its intricate culture-change magic with large national and multinational corporations, the lessons apply equally well to small business.

Top and Bottom

Setting a customer-centric culture starts at the top and reaches the bottom. The leader's example needs to be effective enough that the position on customer experience is understood at every level of the business.

GoDaddy's leadership is clearly setting the right tone, direction and expectations regarding customer experience.

If you're a leader who thinks you can delegate responsibility for customer experience to those managing front-line staff, you'll likely be scratching your head for a while over your low Net Promoter Score®, or NPS.

We love this system. Developed by Fred Reichheld, the NPS revolves around asking clients two simple questions:

1. On a scale of 0 - 10, with 0 being absolutely not and 10 being absolutely yes, would you enthusiastically recommend us as a great brand with which to do business?
2. What is the single biggest reason for that score?

Based on their answers, customers fall into one of just three categories. They are either promoters, neutral, or detractors of your brand. The more promoters you have, the better.

Trust

The most important element of solid client service is trust. You build trust with your clients by honouring confidentiality agreements, operating with transparency, appropriately mitigating risk, and engaging in honest, accountable communication. And you need that trust in order to deliver courageous conversations.

Courageous Conversations

Whether you need to deliver the news that a retail order is late or tell a CEO that his/her decision doesn't align with the strategic imperatives, great customer service includes having courageous conversations... with integrity.

Results

Do what you say you will do. If you're often pumping up promised results in your proposals, worrying about how you'll deliver only after you land the new client, you've got some gaps to fill.

KANDY Outdoor Flooring, for example, has built its culture around a set of core values that includes *deliver on every promise*. This speaks to a leader-driven customer-centric operation that delivers results for the customer. KANDY is doing something right: the brand was a finalist in the 2016 Better Business Bureau Torch Awards.

Create Value

Your aim should be to leave your customers feeling enriched for having done business with you.

At Prompta, Tim Morton reports that often the executive lead for their transformational project will get promoted at the end of the project. That shows they've created value, and the impact is felt well beyond the scope of why they were hired in the first place.

Respect for Culture

Even when Prompta is hired to change the culture, they still go in with respect for the culture that exists.

When doing business with a client, you can share an objective without sharing the same culture. Pay attention to their values, the way they do things, and how they interact. Then blend in.

Here are some stats that help underscore the importance of strong client service in business today:

- How many happy customers are needed to generate eight referrals? Just one. (American Express.)
- How many customers report having switched service providers due to poor customer service? Fifty-two per cent. (Accenture.)
- Customer service is important in the choice of and

loyalty to a brand to what percentage of global
consumers? 97 per cent. (Parature.)

Even though we haven't yet established our Pinnacle Service
Awards, your number one job should be to work for the
nomination.

14

Rock, Paper, Scissors

TECHNOLOGY AND ADMIN

We hired a bookkeeper on the recommendation of a colleague and had been working with her for several months. She wanted us to gather all our paper receipts, print any that were electronic, organize them by both category and month, staple them to pages, and then insert those pages into a binder. When we indicated we were just a little stretched for time, as in too busy, she offered to put the binder together for us. Great!

She was at the opposite end of the country: a three-hour time difference and four Canadian provinces away. With the internet, email and Skype helping us connect, we weren't at all concerned when we hired her.

This binder exercise was a little more than we'd bargained for. Not to let a little logistical detail like geography get in our way, we shipped her all our receipts, and a few weeks later she shipped back a couple of binders along with some instructions on how to add receipts to keep the binder current.

Which we didn't do. The binder sat untouched, except for the dust particles plopping atop and dulling its once shiny surface. We did, however, continue to collect and organize our receipts *electronically*.

Ah, yes. Technology intersects with bookkeeping! If you're not leveraging technology to reduce the time you spend taking care of your money, you're missing out. You're wasting your own time, spending more on bookkeeping and other services than you need, and probably losing new customer opportunities too.

> *Leveraging technology on bookkeeping and administration makes a significant difference and it multiplies efficiency. Paper is becoming less and less relevant in our increasingly digital world. We just don't need it.*
>
> Dara Sklar, Synced With Dara

Sklar's Synced With Dara is where 'digital clutter gets kicked to the curb'. The business launched in 2016 and provides online video training and support to help businesses get rid of paper processes and organize digitally.

Synced With Dara is the result of Sklar's own experience doing the books for her previous business. She was taking eight to ten hours for every month end – the equivalent of one or two days she wasn't available to do billable work for clients. She'd be a week or two into the next month and still hadn't sent out invoices or collected any money. As Sklar says, not good.

Imagine if you were already organized with your bookkeeping 'paperwork'. Then it wouldn't be a big job when it comes time to file taxes or produce reports.

Cloud Storage

The objective is to set yourself up so that you can always find things quickly. One of the key pieces of advice from Dara at Synced With Dara is to use a cloud-based storage system. Dropbox is one great example, but there's also Google Drive, Microsoft's One Drive, and more.

There are four main reasons to choose cloud-based over local computer storage:

- Search functions and security are better in the cloud than they are when locally-based.
- Automatic backups in the cloud mean you don't lose anything from virus attacks, crashes, or theft.
- Does not use your computer's memory, so no matter how much 'stuff' you have filed there, it will not slow you down.
- The ultimate in flexibility, giving you access from anywhere, anytime.

Organizing Files

Once you have your cloud-based system chosen, and you've set up separate personal and business bank accounts, the next step is to organize your electronic folder structure to mirror a well set up physical filing cabinet:

1. Create separate folders for each bank account and credit card associated with your business. If you don't have a business credit card, consider getting one that you use only for business purchases. It could be a separate card altogether, or an additional card on the same account.

The purpose is to be sure you can completely separate business and personal expenditures.

2. Within each account folder, create sub-folders for each monthly statement.

3. Inside that monthly folder, save receipts for all purchases made that month using that account along with the statement for that month.

The behaviour that will really put the cherry on top of your new approach is to adopt a 'touch it once' philosophy. When mail arrives, it gets scanned and saved in the appropriate folder right away. A few minutes each day will save you days of work at month's end.

Ditch Cash

There's not really any need for cash in most businesses today, at least those in advanced and highly regulated economies like Canada. Sure, if your business is a pizza delivery service, you'll want to accept payment in cash. But to pay the business bills, track expenses, invoice customers, and budget? Not needed. Go digital. Paying with a bank or credit card rather than cash means fewer manual entries when you reconcile your expenses.

And go mobile. It's expected today that businesses enable anytime, anywhere payment methods – a clear benefit for customers and also better for you. Less paperwork means more time for you to build your business and generate sales.

Make it Easy for Customers to Pay

Complement your digital move to mobile by making it easy for your customers to pay. Yes, credit card fees can be outrageous, but the easier you make it for people to pay you, the fewer barriers there are to doing business with you.

Use the technology tools available today and watch what happens when you're not buried in paperwork. The world is your oyster when you're digitally organized.

If you simply have a thing for binders, all colour-coded and pretty, can we interest you in an art project?

15

Master or Miner

WHEN TO HIRE HELP

W hen you first start out building your business, long hours and eight-day weeks are expected. You are both quarry master, in charge of the mine, and the miner tunnelling deep underground. However, no one can – or should – keep up that kind of pace forever. It's a drain on your personal, mental, and physical health, and it will kill your business growth.

Doing It All

Sarah Picciotto was a young lawyer in Vancouver, Canada with an entrepreneur's vision. The firms she worked for early in her career, and the lawyers in them, were incredibly busy. They handled their own clients, phone calls and meetings, court appearances and legal drafting, delving into cases, analyzing the law as it applied to each case and then writing about it. Legal research seemed always to be a sore point: not enough time to get it done.

She started OnPoint Legal Research to provide outsourced legal research and writing services to other law firms. And ran smack into the challenge every startup entrepreneur, small business owner or iPro encounters: how long do you keep trying to do everything yourself? When is it right to hire help?

> *When I first started out, I did everything. Pretty soon I had to ask myself the tipping point challenge: is it going to cost me more by way of my time than it would cost to hire someone?*
>
> Sarah Picciotto, OnPoint Legal Research

The first thing Picciotto farmed out was her bookkeeping. She could do it herself, but it made much more sense to farm it out to someone who could do in four hours what would take her eight. Which bought her eight additional hours to allocate to business development. Soon she was also outsourcing her website, design, monthly newsletter, and data entry, and today she outsources as much as she can.

Delegate With Care

Look beyond the typical tasks when you're trying to create some space in your day. Almira Bardai co-founded Jive PR in about 2012. Bardai says the rapid growth of the boutique digital social media and public relations agency delivered important lessons about adding capacity. They started out with a plan that Jive would simply be the two founders providing PR consulting services to clients. They ended up bringing in more business than they expected, and suddenly they needed a people plan to manage their growth.

Bardai and her partner knew they needed to hire people who could do everything the two partners could do. It was the only way the new staff would be able to properly serve the clients on Jive's growing list. Which meant Bardai was hiring for senior, strategic roles.

Jive PR now has offices in Vancouver, Toronto, and California, and was included in the PROFIT/Chatelaine 2016 W100, a program that celebrates entrepreneurial achievement by high-lighting the top 100 women entrepreneurs in Canada. Bardai is now a mentor to others.

> *Many of the women I mentor tend to hire coordinators, which is great. But I ask them: 'how, exactly, are you planning to cut yourself in two?' Because when you're growing a business you need a strategic people plan, and you need to plan for scale. You need to think about replacing yourself.*
>
> Almira Bardai, Jive PR

Know When It's Time

The trick is knowing when the time is right to hire. You don't want to bring on employees, even senior ones, too early or you'll kill your cash flow. Too late and you risk missing that magic market moment because you're just too busy. While the 'right' time will be different for every business, use these parameters as a guide:

- Hire a product design and development lead when you have a team of between one and five people.
- Hire a senior marketing manager once you're working with between five and ten individuals.
- You will probably need a business development and/or sales lead by the time you have 10 to 20 on staff or contract.
- Your operations and HR managers will have plenty to do by the time you're paying between 20 and 50 people.
- Over 50 people? Time to consider bringing on a business intelligence specialist.

There are signposts that indicate when not to hire, too. Feeling stressed and desperate? Don't hire. Mark it down as a learning moment that you needed a better people plan.

When you think you really need help but don't know exactly what the help will do, don't hire. You'll be bringing someone on board who will end up ineffective and confused because you haven't appropriately defined the role or responsibilities.

Ultimately, your responsibility is to the role of quarry master, not miner. Every busy and growing business must, at some point, bring on help.

16

Amethyst or Emerald
DECISIONS, DECISIONS

According to urban (Internet) legend, an adult makes an average of 35,000 decisions every day. Researchers from Cornell University have determined that an adult makes more than 226 decisions every day *about food alone*. Add to that what to wear, stairs or elevator, which bathroom stall, do you call your mother now or later, blue or black pen... and the 35,000 number may not actually be a stretch. Some decisions are precious gems like emerald or semi-precious like amethyst. Still others are more budget-friendly like cubic zirconia or plain pebbles.

As an iPro and entrepreneur, you can be certain your daily decision count is even higher. Running a business of any size means facing a barrage of decisions every day – and sometimes all night. Decisions like: do you exhibit in the trade show? Which size booth? Do you need to cut your operations budget and, if so, how? Which customer lead do you respond to first? Which new manufacturing partner do you go with for your new product? Who do you hire and when? What's the best way to address a customer complaint? What kind of email signature do you want? Do you change brand colours now or do you wait? What blog topic do you write about today? You get the picture. Amethyst or emerald? Decisions, decisions.

A Big Picture View

Every hour of every day as an iPro, entrepreneur or small business owner, you have to decide what to do. In smaller, dynamic environments there often isn't a structure in place to help support the decision making process. There should be.

Start by stepping back and taking a big picture view of your business and where you want it to go.

- What kind of culture do you want for your business?
- What's required to be competitive in your industry?
- Do you want to be innovative or conservative and safe?
- Do you want to empower those around you to become leaders and take initiative?
- Do you want to ensure centralized control?

> *Some people have a greater appetite for moving into the unknown. The more you can establish routines and processes to support decision-making, the more room you create to deal with the big stuff.*
>
> Sharon Ranson, The Ranson Group

Sometimes the big stuff needs a process too. That's our personal experience. When the big stuff comes around in our businesses, and in fact in our lives, we use a matrix that John adapted when he was producing video games at Ubisoft in Montreal.

The Decision Game

John and his 160-member production team were responsible for producing the Xbox, PS2, GameCube, and Wii versions of Tom Clancy's Splinter Cell Double Agent game. Ubisoft's Shanghai office produced the Xbox 360, PS3 and PC versions. Though they shared a similar storyline, there was an element of competition between the two production teams. It was a politically charged time with competing priorities, advancing technology, and big personalities.

While the Shanghai Ubisoft office was freely exploiting the online features of the new Xbox 360, John's team in Montreal struggled with how to mimic the same game play on the older platforms. John's team was faced with the delicate and difficult decision whether to implement the expensive, more technologically-challenged online multi-player feature or a simpler, less expensive, online player-to-player component for Xbox Live.

The question for John was whether it made sense for his team to develop the online game for these older platforms. There were budgetary, creative, and technical impacts that he needed to consider.

John introduced his decision matrix to his team leads and it was invaluable during production of the Splinter Cell game. Suddenly there was a concrete and quantifiable mechanism to support this decision, as well as many others.

Decisions frequently included whether to proceed with items that would cost anywhere from $20k to $200k and whether to use the local Montreal Ubisoft team or farm something out to France. Factors they needed to consider ranged from the impact on user experience and expectations, project timelines, or the effect of loss of creative control.

John's Decision Matrix

We've tried the fishbone decision tool, the decision tree, and a host of other tools designed to help us make better decisions. You'll try a few and come up with the one that works best for you. Here is a sample of the decision making matrix John adapted, and that we use all the time, along with some hypothetical values to demonstrate the point.

Here's how to understand and use the matrix:

1. Down the left-hand side of the matrix are the options on the table.
2. Across the top are the business indicators measured for all potential variations of the project.
3. Weight in per cent is the importance placed on each of the business indicators, and must total 100 per cent regardless of the number of indicators being assessed.
4. Values are how well each option delivers on those business indicators. Cost, in this example, is only weighted at five per cent. A higher number indicates a lower cost, which in this example is more desirable.
5. Each option is scored for a raw value. Each raw value is multiplied by the weighted per cent. In the six-player online option, the cost is fairly undesirable and assessed at a value of two. That is multiplied by the weight of five for a weighted value of 10.

In John's hypothetical example, on the following page, the

highest score of 585 is attributed to the six-player online option. In the real life case of John's work at Ubisoft, the elements were different but the outcome the same. The decision was to proceed with the six-player online option with the Splinter Cell game for the Xbox, PS2, GameCube, and Wii.

Indicators ➤		Cost	Revenue Potential	Time to Develop	Technical Dev.	Total
Weight in %		5%	50%	15%	30%	100%
Options ⌄	Values ⌄					
6-player online	Value (1 – 10)	2	7	5	5	585
	Weighted	10	350	75	150	
Massive multi-player	Value	1	8	2	3	525
	Weighted	5	400	30	90	
Maintain creative plan	Value	8	3	7	7	505
	Weighted	40	150	105	210	

The Impact of Decisions

Decisions in and of themselves are much more powerful than simple elements on a to-do list to be plowed through as quickly as possible and checked off as you go. The decisions you make in your business – even the small ones – affect the people around you, the trajectory your business is on, and the culture of your brand. And the impacts compound over time.

Hence, *how* you make decisions and *who* makes your decisions are every bit as important as *what* those decisions are. Consider the impact on culture of these two differing pieces of advice.

Downside Focus

Tom Anastasi, author of *The Successful Entrepreneur: American Dream Done Right*, recommends that entrepreneurs think of all the possible negative things that could go wrong if you take the decision before you. Anastasi says that if you've looked at everything negative and "you haven't scared yourself off", then it's safe to take the decision to the next step.

Upside Focus

David Reeve of Unleash Culture takes a much different approach from Anastasi. Reeve's position is that looking for negatives first breeds a culture of fear.

> *Many people do indeed operate their businesses from a place of fear. They base their decisions and actions around the what if it goes wrong scenario instead of the what if it goes right scenario.*
>
> David Reeve, Unleash Culture

Neither of these approaches is incorrect, and neither will work for every business.

Here's our bias. Success in business must be first be envisioned. What you think about, you create. By using the downside focus method, you are thinking about all the terrible things that could go wrong. You're engaged in negative visioning and you may unintentionally manifest negative outcomes.

Taking an upside focus does the opposite. You're opening your mind, your being, and your culture to the grand potential of success.

Let Intuition Decide

Intuition is another one of the tools that will work for some entrepreneurs better than others. Those who have heavier doses of intuition and feeling will be more comfortable relying on intuition than those who are more analytical and data-driven. Either way, business decisions are predictive gambles and the facts can only take you so far.

> *The intuitive mind is a sacred gift and the rational mind is a faithful servant. We have created a society that honors the servant and has forgotten the gift.*
>
> Albert Einstein

Entrepreneurs and iPros who work alone are more prone to intuition-error pitfalls: flawed information, emotional bias, prejudice, and inadequate consideration of alternatives. The antidote is a structured decision making process.

17

Meeting Gems

MAKE THEM MATTER

There's a certain sentiment, particularly in the tech startup sector, that meetings are a waste of time. Humbly, respectfully, we call bullshit. We're human beings and, as a species, we function because of our advanced capacity to interact and connect with others. Like during a meeting.

Of course for the busy small business entrepreneur, it's hard enough to squeeze in the time to attend that meeting, never mind find the time to prepare for it in advance and follow up at the end. We get it. However, two of the gems that make every meeting shine are:

1. preparing others to be productive in the meetings you chair, and
2. pre-reading the materials and making connections before the meetings you attend.

Meeting Crashers

We recently watched the movie *The Big Short*, about those few who saw the signs the U.S. housing market was about to take the global economy down with it in the 2008 crash. Actor Steve Carrell plays the obnoxious and neurotic Mark Baum. At one point, Baum walks late into a meeting of his bereavement support group (the character Baum had lost a brother to suicide), still talking on his phone. One participant had been 'sharing' as Baum blustered in. All eyes are on Baum as he sits down noisily in the only empty chair. He closes his flip-phone with a slap and starts to complain loudly about how awful some people are.

"Mr. Baum," the social worker leading the meeting chastises."We've discussed this before. You cannot barge into the meeting and disrupt – "

"I'm not disrupting!" says Baum. "I'm participating." His cell phone rings again. "Sorry, I have to take this," he announces, and walks out. He has disrupted the conversation, derailed the purpose of the meeting, and left everyone else in the room feeling disregarded and frustrated.

Meetings Matter

You'd better hope no one attending your meetings behaves that badly. In truth, there's little anyone could have done to make Baum a productive meeting participant. That doesn't mean you shouldn't try.

As an iPro or freelancer, you likely hold meetings with clients and potential clients. Some of those meetings might be over the phone. If you're running a small business, you might meet with suppliers, stakeholders, and potential partners. As soon as your small business employs people, you'll have internal meetings with the team. And if you're an entrepreneur building a growing concern, you'll have meetings with potential funders, manufacturers, and all the people in the roles above.

Meetings help to:

- align strategy, goals and tactics
- improve accountability and results
- build relationships and trust
- improve communication, and
- provide for social interaction.

If you aren't properly planning every one of your meetings, you might as well be leaving money on the table.

> *Everyone at the meeting has a role to play in making the meeting a productive success. Leaders of and participants in a meeting each share responsibility for its effectiveness.*
>
> Sharon Ranson, The Ranson Group

Leveraging the substance from a well managed meeting requires a bit of a re-think. Ranson promotes thoughtful focus on what happens before, during, and after every meeting.

Before the Meeting

Set a clear purpose. This provides structure and clarity for every attendee to ensure they can contribute what's needed. For example, a meeting's purpose could be to inform, persuade, inspire, decide, motivate, advise, entertain, or refer.

Create the structure for the meeting. Put together an agenda and share it in advance. Schedule an appropriate time of day. Engage with key participants in advance of your meeting to:

- build rapport
- introduce the ideas for the meeting
- communicate the purpose in advance, and
- get early feedback.

Identify your call to action, which could be decisions required or next steps. What do you want each person attending the meeting to do?

During the Meeting

At the start, re-state the purpose of the meeting and the desired outcomes if you know them.

Respect the schedule and timing. If you establish the expectation for an hour-long meeting, it is bad form (and gives rise to the bad reputation meetings have) to let it carry on for three.

Encourage engagement and input. What do participants know? What do they think? What do they need? What do you need to learn?

Then make the call to action. Close the circle and reiterate the purpose of the meeting and the desired outcomes to ensure you accomplished what you came for.

After the Meeting

It isn't over just because the meeting has ended. Send out a summary of the purpose, decisions taken, and action items. Follow up on all the deliverables, continue to engage, and interact with participants to build those relationships. And say thank you!

What about technology? A common trap is mistaking efficiency for effectiveness. It might be more *efficient* to rely on some of the powerful apps or CRM systems to electronically connect with project team members, instead of holding a meeting. However, it's impossible to replace what's lost when you don't have the opportunity to see faces, hear voices, and observe body language. More than 90 per cent of the information absorbed by the brain comes from non-verbal cues and emotional nuance from facial expressions, body language, vocal tone, and pacing. So, if need be, engage with technology to organize the details. If an in-person meeting isn't possible, a virtual, video meeting is better than not holding a meeting at all.

Don't Need a Meeting?

Equally important when planning for effective meetings is the ability to distinguish between circumstances that would benefit from a meeting and those that don't require one.

Use these guidelines to determine whether you really do need a meeting:

- You want to align tasks with objectives.
- You want to paint a common, big picture perspective that goes beyond individual areas of responsibility.
- You can see value in jointly reaching a decision.
- The task at hand requires group collaboration.
- You want to strengthen relationships and build trust.

When you find yourself thinking that meetings are a waste of time, consider it a big flapping red flag. You likely haven't been planning them properly to leverage their power.

If it's your meeting, you are responsible for the planning. Meetings are only a waste of time if you allow them to be.

Yes, it's a busy life and there are a million things to do. Treat your meetings like gems and your staff, stakeholders, partners and customers will notice your shine.

STEP III

To the Moon

18

How's Your Rock Garden

IS GROWTH FOR YOU?

E very new business or iPro venture must initially grow from the seeds of an idea. Some wither at the seedling stage, others hang around happy as a sapling, while still others yearn and strive to reach for the sky. But all types of growth require the same upfront fertilization. With any business, you want to begin with the end in mind.

Gary Prenevost matches those looking to buy a franchise with companies looking for new franchisees. The key is that they are aligned with respect to their personality, style, and goals.

It's not just about income. It's about lifestyle, it's about the team and hours and what kind of work makes them happy. Sixty per cent of franchisees in Canada are not actually interested in growth past a certain point.

The majority of business owners, once they hit a certain stride, are at the fat and happy stage. That's good! You've got what most people go into business for: independence, freedom and control. Why would you want to mess that up?

Gary Prenevost, Franchise Matchmaking Consultant

Tipping Point

What about when you need growth to hit your stride, or when you're actually interested in obtaining and achieving more and better for you and your business?

Remember Pete and Stan from chapter six? They thrive in the fly-by-the-seat-of-your-pants environment. At least they think they do. The truth is, Pete and Stan can make decisions by the seat of their pants for only so long. The same goes for you. There does come a tipping point in every business where you need to have a structure if you want progressive, sustainable growth.

> *Don't be afraid of putting in this structure. It keeps you from chasing the 'shiny objects' that can kill your growth.*
>
> David Reeve, Unleash Culture

Here are Reeve's four tips for a strong growth strategy:

1. Surround yourself with people who like to do things you don't like to do. Get comfortable paying for these services. Understand the difference between spending and investing. If you invest in the services of others, it allows you to spend more time working 'on' your business instead of 'in' your business.

2. Keep it simple. Your strategic plan can fit on one page. Look three years out and reverse engineer what you need to do to get there. Use lead indicators, which we'll describe in a moment, not lag indicators. Track your

progress and results daily so you can make adjustments before it is too late.

3. Be accountable. All excuses are equally bad.
4. Spend as much time telling the character side of your brand story as you do the skill side. Character is what is going to emotionally hook people into your brand. They expect you have skill. They are not expecting to be emotionally hooked.

Lead Indicators

A lead indicator is a predictor of results you'll achieve in the future. It will void your need for a lag indicator report because you'll already know what it's in it. Lead indicators let you track progress toward your goal in real time. If you miss your numbers in week one you can adjust. If you miss your numbers again in week two you still have time to address the problem and adjust. If you miss your numbers in week one, or two, and *don't* address the problem, you won't make your numbers at the end of the month.

Many companies and the people running them rely on lag indicators: reviewing sales and revenue figures for the month, quarter, or year *that has already passed.* By the time they're delivering that report, it's too late to do anything to affect or improve those figures and results.

Lead indicators include things like how many in-person meetings each sales rep holds every week, the number of cold calls to new prospects, and the dollar value of sales required in a particular time period in order to achieve the projected sales targets.

Lead indicators can be influenced on a daily basis. Lead indicators are hot-wired, direct connections between your actions and your goals.

Determining Your Lead Indicators

We were working to develop the franchise model and build the Ontario presence for Vancouver-based KANDY Outdoor Flooring, then a startup brand. Every three or four months we would meet with co-founders Kelly and Doug Niessen in person, either in Vancouver or Toronto. In one of those early meetings, David Reeve was also there, coaching us through the initial setup of our one-page strategic plans. It was a weekend and we'd camped out in the boardroom of a northwest facing office tower in downtown Vancouver. It was February, sunny, cold, and we had a sparkling view of glass-clad high-rise buildings, a million shattered reflections of snow-capped north shore mountains, and the glittering teal blue water of Burrard Inlet. And balconies! So many balconies. KANDY is in the business of providing new outdoor flooring for condo balconies, so this view helped us visualize the potential for our strategic planning session.

Armed with our lag indicators – number of leads by month, number of consultations by month, number of sales and average amount of each sale – we were able to set our lead indicators for the upcoming year.

First, we had to set our goals: how much were we setting out to earn? We needed to establish these targets for each region – Vancouver and Toronto – as well as for the head office, which we were calling KANDY Brand Central, KBC for short.

Hypothetically, let's say our aim was to generate $100,000 in sales in the upcoming fiscal year and that during the previous year an average sale was $2000.

Our numbers told us that for every four leads, we booked one consultation. And for every two consultations, we booked one sale. (That's a 50 per cent close rate!)

- Revenue goal for next year: $100,000.

- Average individual sale: $2,000.
- Total number of sales required to hit revenue goal: 50.
- Number of consultations required to hit 50 sales: 100/2 per week.
- Number of leads required to hit 100 consultations: 400/8 per week.

We were now armed with the knowledge that meant if we did not generate eight new leads and book two consultations each week, we were able to act to get back on track *the very next week.*

No more waiting until the end of the quarter to realize we were off our projections.

Happy With Your Marbles?

Back to those of you who might be happy with your stride, your status quo, your existing bag of marbles. There's nothing wrong with that.

However, you can't just stand still or you will actually lose ground.

Here's what you need to do to protect your position:

- Understand attrition and how you counteract it.
- Understand your customer cycle, customer value, and the length of time they're on board with you.
- Stay educated, informed, and relevant.
- Anticipate and be ready for what's coming next.

So, is it necessary that you drive growth? No. Rock gardens can be beautiful, needing just a little weeding when a bit of green shows through.

But if growth *is* part of your plan?

Cultivate the fertile soil between the rocks, with a little structure for the growth of your small business, and turn your rock garden into a blossoming riot of colour.

19

Peak Productivity
EFFICIENCY & PROFITS

Aiming for peak productivity is not just a game for number nerds (a term of endearment!). When your business is able to produce goods and services more efficiently, increasing productivity, it leads to a stronger competitive position, increased revenues and profits, and higher quality goods and services. And it will open the door to new business opportunities.

Productivity is a performance indicator that, in its simplest form, is a calculation of the ratio between the added value in dollars and the labour hours required to produce that value.

There are several ways to grow. Adding people to your payroll is one kind of growth. Increasing sales and revenue is another. Often one will lead to the other. Neither of those, on their own, will necessarily pad your pockets with profits. If you don't have a handle on your productivity, your expenses will increase at the same pace, or more, and you will be no farther ahead.

Remember Jackson Manonell from chapter 12? He's now been on the job with Starbucks a year and has been promoted to shift supervisor. The slick, customer-centric and friendly environment of Starbucks camouflages the sales and productivity machine at work behind the counter.

Jackson dons his green Starbucks apron and affixes his personally-designed name tag. It's the beginning of his shift and the first thing he does is check each cash terminal for its sales data: number of customers and total dollars sold, broken down by half-hour. He checks labour hours so far, looks at the labour hours still to come in terms of who is scheduled to work the remainder of the day, and does a calculation of the labour hours against the sales.

If it's been a really busy day, meaning high sales volume in comparison to labour hours, Jackson has the option to call in additional staff. This would help ensure a consistent customer experience by propping up the bench strength, and it also helps keep the productivity in balance.

If it's been a really slow day, meaning a low sales volume in comparison to labour hours, Jackson has the option of sending one or more baristas home early.

It is just as important for an iPro or freelancer to keep their eyes on productivity as it is for a behemoth like Starbucks. Your productivity can be improved, for example, through training and targeting your marketing spend better. Don't waste time trying to attract people who aren't in your target audience. Don't tear your hair out trying to retain an unhappy customer that is taking extra hours of your time and making you miserable in return.

There are four overall indicators that help you keep an eye on your productivity health:

- revenue per person in your organization
- profit per person in your organization
- labour productivity, and
- capital productivity.

And there are six key ways you can improve productivity.

1. Measure. Measuring productivity is the first step to improving productivity. You might think you're as productive as possible, but measuring often reveals opportunities for improvement you didn't know were there.

2. Trim. Once you start measuring your productivity, you will soon see where you have an opportunity to trim and tighten up. Overproduction, waiting, transport, inefficient operations, holding more inventory than you can sell in a single season, unnecessary motion in your processes and systems, poor quality, and poor design are all areas prone to wastage.

3. Train. Training and development budgets are often the first to be trimmed during an economic downturn or in tough times. However, from a productivity perspective, that's a counterproductive move. When times are tough is precisely when you want to motivate and equip your people to perform with optimum efficiency. A number of studies conclude that training – both general and specific – ranks higher than investment in new equipment for increasing productivity.

4. Improve. Improve the processes for operations management. You can choose to pursue a continuous improvement approach such as Lean certification, hire a consultant to help you re-engineer, or establish an internal team to examine and recommend process improvements for all of your operations.

5. Develop. Extend the continuous improvement approach to your suite of products and services. Can you improve your current offerings? What new products or services can you develop to introduce to the market?

6. Invest. The investments that make the biggest impacts on productivity are those in information and communications technology. Lack of technological currency will leave a company – or an iPro – lagging well behind its competitors.

Remember that there are several ways to grow. Let your inner number nerd loose and keep an eye on the ratio between your labour hours and your added value to ensure your expenses don't keep pace. Peak productivity means profits. Who doesn't dream of more profits?

20

Ditch the Boulders

BYE-BYE BAD CUSTOMERS

Have you ever had that feeling when you're communicating with a potential new client that they are going to be trouble? It's like they fill your pockets with boulders and you start tumbling head over heels down a steep hill. And then you proceed to do business anyway?

John learned this lesson the hard way when he was co-owner of Montage Multipiste, a Montreal-based sound studio.

A client needed sound editing for his movie. It was a huge job, good for the bottom line and the sound studio's list of credits. But something about the guy didn't sit well with John. He wasn't sure what, and he couldn't say why, but the fit did not feel right.

Because the work was interesting and the money was good, he went ahead anyway. The contract stipulated a payment plan and a project delivery timeframe. The finished and edited audio would be delivered to the client in sections as they were complete.

The Devil's in the Details

Sound editing is a detail job. Audio specialists like John could easily spend a whole day on one minute of audio. And so delivering a reasonably sized audio section for the film every two weeks was plenty. John delivered one section to the client about a week before Christmas and got right to work on the next.

The day before Christmas, out of the blue, the client called and demanded that the rest of the project be delivered the next day. The. Next. Day! There was at least four days' work that needed to be crammed into the next 24 hours, and it was Christmas Eve.

These were in the early days of business ownership for John. Had he been more seasoned, he may have calmly pulled out the contract and explained that on-demand delivery on Christmas Day wasn't in there. He would have pointed out that the project was on track and on time. Then he would have packed up the office, and gone home to celebrate Christmas with his family. Or better yet, he would have recognized his early discomfort with this client and not accepted the job in the first place.

But it *was* early days in John's business ownership life. So, he pulled an all-nighter, worked all through Christmas Day, and delivered the final section of the film's sound just before midnight on the 25th. He was angry and upset, and sad to have missed the family festivities. But he finished and got paid for the project. And vowed never to work with that client again.

Was giving in to the client's unreasonable demands simply the price of being in business? Or did it cross the line, costing more on the personal side than it was bringing in on the business side? There's no clear-cut answer to that one. It often depends: on the circumstances, the ability of the business to absorb the loss should the client decide not to pay, and the history with that client.

There are many shifts in mindset that occur for the business owner between the crazy, adrenaline and hope-fuelled startup phase and business maturity. But none is as powerful as moving from needing to accept any and all business to only attracting – and keeping – the right business.

> *A good business relationship is like any relationship. It has to be a two-way street and mutually beneficial. If the relationship is not working, either party should be able to end it as long as they are following the terms of the contract.*
>
> Ilan Cooley, Loud Mouth Communications

In 2004 Ilan Cooley started Loud Mouth Communications, specializing in public relations, sponsorship and event management for lifestyle and entertainment clients. Cooley has learned that as a business owner you get to pick – you must pick – who hires you.

Here are four key ways to reduce the risk of you ending up at odds with a client:

- Know your business goals, objectives, model and values and select clients who are a match.
- Develop a solid service or sales contract that includes payment terms, copyright and intellectual property rights, and a termination clause. It should also support how you work and how you expect to be treated by clients.
- Set rates or prices that adequately reflect the quality of your products or services. The temptation to low-ball the competition can backfire and bring problematic clients out of the woodwork.

- Ensure you have tight scope documents that go into detail about project boundaries, milestones, and the level of contribution required from you and the client. Some small business service providers find that merging the contract, proposal and scope documents helps eliminate confusion.

But no matter how careful you are with the steps above, it's not a guarantee. Sometimes things just don't work out and you have to end the relationship.

> *I do sometimes have to fire a bad customer: when they want more than I can provide, which means simply that they are increasing my costs through inefficient use of my time.*
>
> Ellen Varner, E-Trademark Universe

Varner's business is all online. Her efficiency is how she guarantees service standards and turnaround times in her global trademarking business.

Numbers Don't Lie

If you're not sure whether you're just having a bad day or your client may indeed be a problem, remember that numbers don't often lie.

You'll develop a better understanding of how each customer relationship impacts your profitability when:

- your accounting system attributes both revenue and costs to each customer
- you are able to assign cost of goods sold (COGS) and

acquisition costs, including direct marketing to each customer and customer group
- you can track the time you – and your staff, if applicable – spend serving and retaining each customer, and
- you can compare the revenue/cost ratio for each customer.

The numbers will usually support what you already know in your gut. Still, it can be difficult to think about turning revenue away, especially in the early days of a business when every penny counts.

> *I decided to pick clients and projects based on wanting to deliver results, not just for the money. For me the stress of having to work in a negative environment is not worth it.*
>
> Ilan Cooley, Loud Mouth Communications

Taking all possible measures to attract the right clients, and paying attention to your internal responses when first negotiating with new ones, will help keep you in business relationship heaven. Until they don't.

Pay attention to that feeling of your pockets filling up with rocks. Turn them out before they take you down with them.

Breaking up with bad clients may be tough, but you will clear away the clutter and the negative energy that lies in the path of your success. The sooner you can make that shift, the better off you and your business will be.

21

Promote the Jewels

MARKETING STRATEGY

B efore you can promote the jewels, you need to be sure that you've actually got jewels. That means doing everything with a marketing lens.

One of the biggest mistakes new entrepreneurs and iPros make is to underestimate the power and importance of marketing. Right from the earliest days of a startup, it deserves a seat with the big boys: finance, HR, operations, product development and sales. It should not be an afterthought.

Marketing is more than simply driving traffic, online advertising, and flooding people's email inboxes with promos. It is also understanding your customer segments and your unique value proposition (UVP). It's how well you tell your story as well as what you're selling.

Marketing's 4Ps – product, price, place and promotion – are a core part of the business strategy. This chapter isn't to educate you on the 4Ps, rather to help you ensure you're considering them in all you do.

Market Research

As a business owner, you're conducting market research all the time, whether you're aware of it or not. Every time you talk about your business to a prospective customer, or check out the offerings and prices of your competitors, you're engaged in market research. However, you'll need to be systematic about collecting and recording your findings. Especially when you start out.

> *Most entrepreneurs start out because they're passionate, they have a hunch, they sense the market is there. But at a certain point as a business owner you have to stop and figure out how to invest in market research.*
>
> Ravi Dindayal, Business Development Bank of Canada (BDC)

For DIY market research, you may not find a lot of good quality secondary information. Governmental statistics agencies, such as Statistics Canada, can be a good and reliable source. You can hire a market research firm which can quickly become expensive or you can use an online survey tool like SurveyMonkey. Put together a list of 30 people you think might fit your customer profile, including friends and family, and ask them a series of questions designed to provide insights into the market related to your products and services.

When Kelly and Doug Niessen were germinating their new outdoor flooring business idea, they conducted a lot of their market research before they knew it was market research. As consumers, they were looking for a way to beautify their own condo balcony. And they couldn't find anyone offering either the products (outdoor flooring) or the services (design, delivery, installation) they wanted.

They backed up that personal research with statistics on housing starts, owner-occupied condominiums, and the growth in the number of people choosing condo living over single family homes.

What did they learn? There was a critical mass of potential customers and no one out there serving the need.

Attracting the 'Right' Customer

You've no doubt heard the saying 'the customer is always right'. In today's digital marketing world, it is 'the *right* customer is always right'. Dindayal says it is common for businesses, regardless of how big the business is, to lack an understanding of their high value customers. You want to ensure your limited resources are targeting the right customers.

Identifying those high value customers requires a dashboard system of key performance indicators (KPI). It doesn't have to be fancy, a series of Excel spreadsheets will do. You'll want to collect data that tell you how much time and money you're spending on a customer and compare it to what they've signed up for.

A customer that spends eight dollars per month with you and takes up eight hours of your time every month? That's a customer to send to your competition.

Marketing Strategy vs. Marketing Plan

Don't confuse a marketing strategy with a marketing plan. They're different beasts, with different purposes.

Marketing strategy provides you with a roadmap to accomplish your business objectives and achieve results, like better market penetration and sales growth. It is a collection of medium-term and long-term methods that won't change year over year, unless something major changes, like legislation, a big new competitor, or a shift in consumer behaviour. And it helps ensure you're focusing resources to attract employees, partners and customers using only those initiatives that support your overall business objectives.

You'll recall in chapter six there is a section on marketing in your business plan. The market analysis, segmentation, competition and pricing form the basis of your marketing strategy, and you'll add your business marketing objectives along with the broad approaches you'll adopt to achieve those objectives over a fairly long term: 12 - 24 months.

A marketing plan is a collection of the marketing tactics and initiatives you'll implement for a specific initiative, or for the given period – monthly, quarterly, or annually. It changes at least annually to address opportunities, threats, and competitive actions, and it includes budgets, deadlines, and well-defined responsibilities. In your marketing plan, you'll complete the following sections:

- objective of the initiative
- target market and key demographics
- key messages
- call to action
- process, list development, prospecting method
- event details, if applicable
- rollout or gantt chart
- budget, and
- metrics, expectations and how you'll measure success.

Back to KANDY Outdoor Flooring. A big part of the marketing strategy in the first five years involved educating consumers that they had options to spruce up their outdoor spaces. Because no one had previously been operating in this market niche, most people didn't even know they wanted new outdoor flooring for their condo balconies. It took a concerted effort. Kelly and Doug attended major home and garden trade shows, conducted influencer outreach, and engaged in targeted marketing activities. Now that the consumer has caught on (and so have the copycat businesses, but that's another story), their strategy can shift.

Marketing as Differentiator

Are you giving marketing the respect it deserves? Look around your business and ask yourself how you've been treating marketing: as a fluffy afterthought or fundamental pillar?

Successful companies are led by entrepreneurs that have their marketing hats on from the beginning. They understand that marketing is an essential part of the business strategy.

They know they've got precious jewels. They polish them to a brilliant gleam and promote the heck out of them.

22

Polish Your Granite

CREATE BRAND CONTENT THAT SHINES

Y ou've been to those homes: the granite kitchen countertop is
so smooth and shiny that when you bend over it, you see
your own face smiling back. That's the effect you want with your
brand content: a pure, honest reflection of your brand, targeted to
the customer who sees himself in it.

Your brand content is the emotional connection that converts a
consumer into a customer. More than 80 per cent of consumers are
researching – and shopping – online. They're hiring online, too. So,
thinking strategically about how your content positions and reflects
your brand personality is key.

What Do We Mean, Content?

Think of content as the new advertising. In the heady days depicted
on the Mad Men television series, for example, when men domi-
nated and advertising ruled, great ad campaigns used to be the best
way to get your message out to consumers.

Today, it's all about content. Creating, sharing and promoting information that is consistent, relevant and of value to a defined audience. Done well, content opens the door to a relationship with the consumer that breeds loyalty and, ultimately, profitability.

Your content includes everything you write on your website, your blog, guest blogs, or media articles. It is every video, email signature, voice mail message, and social post. And it is your business proposal, sales quote, invoice, and payment receipt.

Authenticity and Alignment

Jesse Royce was over-the-moon thrilled to be realizing her dream. She quit her nine-to-five job, and hung out her shingle, so to speak, and started Jesse's Journey, a weight loss coaching business. She had her own successful weight loss to showcase, having lost 125 pounds 10 years ago and kept it off. With her coaching certification, she was ready to take on clients.

Jesse's Journey offered in-person coaching services as well as on-line video call coaching to people in London and around the world. The only restriction was that they speak English.

Jesse vowed to 'do it right', too. She hired a professional writer to generate the website content and to write the first six months' worth of blogs. She envisioned a sophisticated look and feel, and directed the writer accordingly. Jesse wanted to attract a particular type of client, sophisticated, wealthy and educated, and she believed her website would help her do that.

The first challenge was that Jesse wasn't like her ideal client. She didn't have any post-secondary education. Born, raised, and still living in the east end of London, Jesse's speech patterns were distinctively cockney. For example, she pronounced the 't's' between vowels with a glottal stop, which means the word 'better' comes out as 'be'uh.

One of her first in-person client sessions was booked online and confirmed via email. Jesse and Emma had exchanged all the relevant details without actually speaking. When Jesse arrived, rang the bell, and walked up to the first floor flat, she couldn't help but quiver with excitement. Her first client! In a good neighbourhood!

But when the door of the flat opened, Emma's round face peering through a small crack before opening wider, things changed.

"Good day, I think I'm at the right place," said Jesse, extending her hand. What that sounded like was "good die, I fink I'm at vuh roi-ut place".

Emma looked shocked and couldn't speak for several seconds. This was not the person she expected from the look and feel of the Jesse's Journey website. She expected someone more... someone not from the east end.

There's nothing wrong with a cockney accent, but it is most often spoken by the working class. Not by Emma. And not by the sophisticated, wealthy class of Brit that Jesse was hoping to attract to her weight loss coaching business.

Jesse's Journey is a brand whose personality and character is absolutely going to reflect the personality and character of Jesse, the founder. Jesse's Journey is Jesse. By contrast, a larger business with an executive team and many staff can often have a brand personality created specifically to connect with a target audience.

What Jesse needed to do was showcase her passion, compassion, personal experience, and capacity to coach others through behaviour change. Then she needed to develop a content strategy that would help her to connect with her sophisticated target audience. Instead, she tried to *be like* her target audience, which backfired because it wasn't authentic.

How do you create brand content that resonates with your audience

and is an authentic reflection of your brand values and personality?
Follow these five steps.

1. Understand Your Audience

You already have a market identified for your business. Now it's
time to really get to know your audience.

- What are their interests?
- What do they do with their leisure time?
- Are you clear on their expectations, their wants and their
  needs?
- How do they talk?
- Where are they online?

You also want to get familiar with their values. If you discover
your audience's values do not align with your own, it may be time
to go back to the drawing board. Your audience is comprised of
more than customers or potential customers. Also consider stakeholders, influencers, and brand promoters as members of your
audience.

Listen to your audience. And when you create brand content be
sure it helps address what they want and what they need. This may
or may not be directly related to what you sell.

2. Get Clear on Your Brand Personality

A brand's personality is usually an extension of the leader's personality. That is, unless there is a strategic reason to create one that is
different. Is your brand casual or conservative? High-tech and edgy
or traditional? Fun or formal? A great example of a brand that
exploded onto the market and immediately made its brand personality part of its appeal is WestJet, a Canadian airline company

started in 1996 to rival conventional players Air Canada and now-defunct Canadian Airlines, which closed its doors in 2001. Entering the challenging and competitive space of commercial airlines, WestJet infused all its brand content with vigour, humour, and informal connections. It was the first North American airline to write casual, often funny scripts for the flight attendants to deliver during the safety demonstrations. Customers loved it.

3. Establish Your Voice and Tone

Connect your voice and tone to both your audience and your brand personality. Your voice includes the fun or formal elements of your brand personality along with any specific words or phrases you use to describe your products or services. Your voice will remain constant across all content platforms and conversations, but your tone reflects an attitude and will shift with the purpose of each message.

4. Roll it Up into a Brand Guide

Your brand guide will contain all of the information above, as well as guidelines around your logo, use of trademarks, and tag lines. It can even have a suggested 'elevator pitch'. It will guide each member of your team in speaking to and writing for your audiences, internal and external, in a way that remains consistent. And consistency is key for maintaining quality standards and protecting your brand's identity.

5. Include ALL Your Content

Your brand content extends well beyond your website and Facebook ads. In Jesse's case, after going back to the drawing board on her web content, she rolled that personality through to her email signature, her sales quotes, her invoices, and her recorded voicemail message. You want to infuse all your content with your brand personality.

If your content is not an authentic representation of your small business, people will pick up on that. It's like a sniff test, and even if your intentions are pure you will come off as insincere.

If your content is just like everyone else's out there, you're telling the world there is nothing different or special or unique about you.

If your content is different from one platform (website) to another (sales quote), your brand will seem schizophrenic with a split personality. You will be giving potential paying customers an inconsistent experience with your content, leading them to think they might be in for inconsistent experiences as a customer. And so they go elsewhere. Probably not what you want.

As soon as you have more than one person responsible for creating brand content, it becomes more difficult to ensure voice and tone are consistent. Having a detailed brand guide that you share, train on, and keep updated will go a long way to helping you maintain consistency.

Be purposeful about creating content that accurately reflects your brand personality, like the reflection of your face in that gleaming granite counter. That's how you'll connect emotionally with your ideal customer. And that's how to ensure your sales and success will grow.

23

Trade Show Rock Star

TIPS & TRICKS FOR THE EXHIBITION

With so much business being done online, you'd think the trade show business would be flagging. Not so. People still crave that personal touch: the ability to look someone in the eye and read their body language when they are making their pitch. Do this well and you can be the rock star of every trade show in which you exhibit.

Level Playing Field

Exhibiting at a trade show immediately levels the playing field between you and your competitors, no matter how much bigger or richer or more established they are. Every business pays essentially the same per-square-footage rate (for similar traffic locations) to get in front of people who are ready – or getting ready – to buy.

Nestled into the foothills east of the towering Rocky Mountains just northwest of Calgary, Alberta, is the Canadian town of Cochrane. It's ranching roots are displayed with street names like Cowboy Trail and Star Ranch Road. It's where cattle rancher Kathy McDonald lives and where she started an unlikely business.

Her partner had been taking hunting trips to Africa for several years. McDonald went along a couple of times, started taking a few people along with her, and suddenly she had this: Extreme Outdoor Safaris.

Word of mouth and personal networking have always been the most effective way for McDonald's guided African hunting and photographic adventure tours business to develop new client relationships. Setting up booths at trade shows and exhibitions seemed a perfectly natural extension of what was already happening: conversations with people interested in a guided trip to Africa.

> *Our trade show objective is not so much about getting direct sales at the show. We do the trade shows to build relationships over a longer term.*
>
> Kathy McDonald, Extreme Outdoor Safaris

Planning and executing a successful trade show appearance takes some work, even if you're not you're lugging in boxes of widgets you hope to sell or building a complex booth. After several years exhibiting and presenting at oodles of national, international and regional trade shows, both in Canada and the U.S., we have developed our own best practices.

Show Strategy

It starts with choosing the right show for your business's target market. Choose shows with the largest attendance (of the right audience, of course), the best industry reviews, and biggest ad spend. Articulate your sales strategy to those helping staff your booth and offer what attendees want. Set objectives. This could be number of units sold, leads generated, trips booked.

Care and Feeding

Be prepared to eat and drink trade show talk for the duration, and, yes, to be exhausted. Plan healthy snacks, bring water. Taking care of you first will help your clients feel your positive energy output. Don't eat at the booth: first, it signals you are not ready to engage; second, you'll be smiling at the most important prospect of the year with a hunk of leafy green stuck between your teeth. Eeew.

Attract and Engage

A professional, orderly booth with visual, audio, video, printed materials, and product samples will draw and hold interest. Open, engaging staff wearing branded clothing will help ensure you're providing an amazing client experience. And it will set the tone for every other client touch point throughout your relationship.

Capture and Convert

You will need tools to capture lead information: pen and paper, computer, tablet, or other technology that won't fail when you can't take the time to fix the glitch.

Shorten the gap between expression of interest and sale whenever possible. Here's what we did while working with KANDY Outdoor Flooring and its National Home Show booth. KANDY's sales process involves in-home consultations, so our strategy was to close the gaps between:

1. an expression of interest,
2. booking a consultation, and
3. the actual consultation and sale.

Before the show even started, we created a list of available time slots that would allow us to schedule a consult with a prospect on the spot. We didn't make them wait until after the show, either. We set up early morning and evening appointments on show days.

The National Home Show in Toronto is a big 10-day show with hundreds of exhibitors and nearly 200,000 attendees. In our first year we left much of the lead follow-up and consultation scheduling until after the show ended. By then, some people had forgotten who we were. We never made that mistake again.

Giveaways vs Gimmicks

Giveaways should relate directly to your products or business. Don't give away candy unless you're a candy business. It might draw people to your booth but they will not remember you and it's a waste of money.

Trade Show Etiquette

It's wonderful to be enthusiastic, but have the good graces to recognize when your competitor is legitimately engaged with a prospect. Don't interrupt. You're impressing no one – especially not that potential customer – with your aggressive behaviour.

Follow Up

Even if you created an amazing client experience at your booth, the memory of your business will fade, so connect with leads as soon as possible. If you want to be a trade show rock star, remember it's a numbers game. Another "no thanks" increases the odds the next person will say "let's do it".

24

Launch Your Landslide
WHEN A BOOK BOOSTS BUSINESS

W riting a book can be a great way to launch your landslide and boost your business.

We're not talking about the catastrophic landslide that will bury you under tons of rock. We're referring to the landslide that unleashes a torrent of new customers, speaking engagements, accolades, and credibility from corners of your mountain you didn't even know existed.

There are independent authors – we call them authorpreneurs – whose *business* revolves around writing, publishing, marketing, and selling books.

Other nonfiction authors write books that are *about* their main business. Like David Reeve, whose book is about helping other startups build strong cultures that accelerate the growth of their brands.

Why Write a Book?

There are many great reasons to write a book, and any one or more might be a fit for you. Many people write books to make an argument for a social, environmental, economic, or political cause. Others are driven to write that award-winning historical novel set in ancient times. And still others are bursting at the seams with the story of their family's epic migration across oceans as they flee war, famine, genocide, poverty, or pursue simple dreams of a better life.

The motivation for writing a book for your business is a little different, even though some of the outcomes may be the same. While you need just one solid 'why' that resonates with you and makes sense for your business, it's common for more than one of the following categories to be a fit:

- You want to help other people.
- You want to establish yourself as an authority on your subject and raise your visibility.
- You are starting, running or growing a business around the topic and you want to generate interest and attract clients.
- You are passionate about the topic and want to get it out to the world.
- You are looking to switch careers or industries and think the book can help.

Books That Convert

Colin Campbell, a marketing and sales copywriter with a flair for language that engages, started Books That Convert to create books for business people interested mainly in generating more leads.

> *After working on about seven books for authors, I realized*

there was a formula that no one else was using. I created this awesome method to write and produce a book for them in 30 days. It works.

Colin Campbell, Books That Convert

We first met Colin the week we were leaving Canada back in 2015. Just four days, in fact, before we left Toronto, moved to Mexico, and bought our 40' sailboat. We were in Starbucks, sitting at a 4' x 12' dark wood table. The coffee was good, the music was pleasant, and our table was full of computers clack-clacking as others wrote or programmed or played games.

As John and I discussed something between us, this friendly fellow sitting directly across from us chimed in. Soon we were having a most engaging three-way conversation.

We connected in a way that was unusual for us. We're entrepreneurs and know how to go after what we want, but we're both still introverts at heart. Having chatted for a total of an hour, Colin invited us to his home for dinner.

Incredulous, both at the invite and our open response, we accepted. We enjoyed a fantastic evening of good healthy food and great conversation. We bade adieu that night and, because we were moving to a new country, we didn't really expect to see or hear from Colin again.

We had, however, connected on Facebook. Which is how we learned that a few months after our departure from Canada, perhaps inspired by our sailboat adventures, Colin also departed, driving across Canada and down the West Coast of the United States in a small van. About 18 months after that first meeting and dinner, when our planning for the launch of Ingenium Books was in full swing, we saw a Facebook post from Colin that we couldn't ignore:

> *When you experience my interview process, you'll know why it's ground-breaking. So why should YOU care about any of this? I want 5 - 12 people to join me in a case-study group to go through my book-production system. You'll get your book done in less than 60 days, using only 3 - 5 hours of your time chatting with me.*

Colin Campbell, Books That Convert

We knew Colin was a kick-ass copywriter, but *books* are a different beast. We didn't know if he already had a team ready to help him with these editorial projects. So we got in touch and offered our assistance editing and formatting the five books in his case study. We helped Colin confirm that his Books That Convert premise was workable: it *is* possible to produce a short nonfiction lead magnet book from start to finish in 30 days. For business people who put a priority on the length of time it takes to produce a short book, this is brilliant.

These Books That Convert aren't heavily filled with research or technical details. Each covers the problem the author and his/her business solves, their personal journey with the topic of the book, and then the fairly high-level solution. Readers interested in learning more are encouraged to reach out to the author and engage him/her through coaching services, for example, to join social media groups and email lists, and in general support the author with new business.

Colin's approach is ideal for those looking for a quick turn-around book when their main objective is to generate leads. This is one way to write a book that benefits your business, but it isn't the only way. Sometimes you need to put more into a book – more research, more detail, more time, and yes, more money. And you can get more back, too.

What if you have larger aspirations? What if you want to change the world, whether or not it brings you more business? What if you've accomplished something great, or mastered a personal challenge, and you want to share your story to help motivate others?

Change the world

You may want to change the world and writing your book is how you'll do it. Or you may have already changed the world and the book is the story of how you've done it. Either approach can be micro or macro: changing the world one person at a time or changing the world in a global way. Let's look at both.

Micro change

Lauren Clucas is a South African relationship counsellor who wants to change the world – one couple at a time – by helping them create a really strong relationship. Healthy relationships are tied to physical health and longer lives. Lauren wanted to share the concepts she developed over the more than a decade working with couples in Singapore, Australia, and South Africa.

> *I recognised that some couples, regardless of the drama, conflict or disharmony between them, engaged certain qualities which enabled them to push through and thrive, while others, sometimes with relatively less adversity, chose to divorce or part ways. I became curious about couples that thrived in the wake of adversity. They found ways to want the relationship and to make each other feel wanted in the relationship.*

Lauren Clucas, author

Lauren's unique concepts involved opponents, intruders, and allies, and the more she used the concepts in closed-door sessions as she worked to illuminate the behaviours and skills needed for a relationship that really works, the more she realized she wanted everyone to benefit. Her main aim is to change the world with her book: to make it easier for people struggling in their primary love relationships to experience a fulfilling, rewarding, lasting, and healthy bond.

Lauren came to Boni and Ingenium Books looking for an editor and they worked together across continents thanks to video call technology. They fleshed out ideas, reworked and reordered some of the content, ultimately fine tuning and finalizing the manuscript. *Wanted: How to Create a Relationship That Really Works* is now available for purchase on Amazon.

Lauren is changing the world on a micro level, literally one person or couple at a time. More happy marriages mean better health outcomes and lower government expenditures on health, fewer crimes of passion, etcetera.

Macro change

Then there is change on a global scale. Mark Zuckerberg's Facebook is social technology that has dramatically changed how we relate to one another on both a personal and a global scale. Steve Jobs's Apple created both hardware and software platforms that changed the way we work and interact – and Jobs did write a book before he died, too young, from cancer.

Mastering a challenge

When John, co-author of *Rock Your Business*, was training Ontario realtors on the use of GeoWarehouse, the online land registry service developed and offered by Teranet, he was a featured presenter at more real estate trade shows than he can remember. At one of them, John's presentation followed Marnie McBean, a three-time Olympic gold medallist, recipient of the Order of Canada, and author. Her book, *The Power of More, How Small Steps Can Help You Achieve Big Goals*, teaches readers how to break every goal into smaller bite-sized pieces and then *go for more*. At this particular trade show, all attendees received a free copy of McBean's book, which detailed her journey from a young teen turning the impossibility of competing in rowing at the Olympic level into a challenge she overcame and mastered. These scenarios make great and inspirational stories.

Here are some other ways your business book could fit into this 'mastered a challenge' category:

- You've weathered a bankruptcy and bounced back to build a thriving, successful business.
- Your own version of rags to riches (think Colonel Sanders who used a social security check to start Kentucky Fried Chicken).
- You've recovered from a serious injury or other health setback and your business is thriving anyway.
- You've developed a unique or proprietary system or approach to a common problem that solves it in a special way.

What a book will NOT do

You'll notice when we've been discussing what a book could do for your business – build credibility, generate leads, bring in new business – two concepts are missing. Writing and publishing a book will not:

- make you rich, or
- make you famous.

Writing and publishing a book – a single book – isn't enough to make you special just for that fact. If you're already rich and famous, and then you write a book, you can expect a decent volume of sales. But that's because people are buying your book because you're already famous, not necessarily because they actually care about your book. If you're not famous, like us, and you write a book, like us, you can expect your life to change very little indeed. Unless, of course, you write many books, or build a business around books like we have.

To summarize, here is what writing a book can do for your business:

- Build credibility & enhance your reputation.
- Help you change and improve the world.
- Help others overcome a challenge.
- Grow your email list, social following, and web traffic.
- Get new clients & referrals.
- Generate speaking engagements.
- Sell some books!

The digital revolution is democratizing the book publishing industry the same way it did with the sound production and video industries. The tools make it easy to do it yourself from your basement or living room. You don't even need a publisher anymore. You can go direct to Amazon, or Kindle, or any of the other digital or print-on-demand book distributors. You can write it yourself, hire a good editor, craft your own book cover or hire a book cover designer, or you can hire help for any or every stage.

This is what Ingenium Books does. We make it easy for indie authors to write, edit and publish their books. Find out more about us by visiting our website at www.ingeniumbooks.com.

―――――

Consider whether writing a book might help you launch your own business landslide. Might it let loose a flood of new clients, bring in speech requests, make you the popular dinner guest, and get you the credibility you know you deserve?

25

Earthquake Blues

TAKE A BREAK OR BREAK DOWN

F irst you take big ideas and small pockets, add long to-do lists and a lack of help. Mix with 12 to 18 hours a day running full throttle as you juggle the demands of HR, accounting and budgeting, sales, customer service, webmaster, and marketing. Soon you'll experience a rumbling of the earth beneath your feet, so gentle at first you might miss the signs, reverberations travelling up into your very core. Keep mixing those ingredients without taking a break and soon you risk experiencing the full-blown earthquake blues. Also known as a breakdown.

If you're one of those small business entrepreneurs who feels the pinch and pressure of time and you don't take breaks for yourself, you are on a slippery slope toward ineffectiveness or worse, a health crisis.

We've been there, too. When John owned his sound production studio, Montage Multipiste in Montreal, he was responsible for sales and production and mixing and maintenance and money and working 18 hours a day was absolutely normal. Until he ended up in hospital with stress-related health issues and he saw the damage he was doing.

Early in her television reporting career, Boni fed the adrenaline monster while working at a station in Prince George, B.C., producing and hosting a daily live talk show at 9:30 a.m. then anchoring live newscasts at noon, 3:00 and 5:00 p.m. Her boss, Mike Woodworth, would tell her she needed to get out of the news-room for a break mid-day. She rarely did. Years later, the habit firmly entrenched from 15 years as a journalist always on deadline, attending murder scenes and covering organized crime and politics and business, Boni was diagnosed with fibromyalgia, a stress-related autoimmune disorder.

But you're strong as an ox, right? Your health and your immune system can hold up to that degree of constant pounding and self-driven pressure, right? That may be. But by not taking a break you're harming your business, too.

> *When you're on at work too long for too often, you drain your energy reserves—like a battery—and need to recharge. The brain becomes fuzzy, unable to focus, the body becomes lethargic, and the soul becomes numb.*
>
> Cynthia Barlow, C3 Conversations

Operating a business while your brain and body are in this suppressed state will affect your ability to make sound decisions. You won't be able to step back out of the day-to-day minutiae to think about the big picture, to set your vision and strategy, or plan for the future.

The No Grow Zone

How do you know you're in this no-grow zone, simultaneously doing too much (at work) and doing too little (no breaks)? Here are a few signs and symptoms:

- You feel anxiety, first related to a specific thing and then generally, when you can't pinpoint a direct cause.
- You start waking up in the wee hours of the night with worry or stress.
- You lose your sense of joy, your joie de vivre.
- You lose your sense of humour.
- Once a master multi-tasker, you start losing track of the status of projects.
- Your decisions turn out poorly or backfire.
- You rely more and more on several shots of espresso to get you through the day.
- You are too busy to take a break.

We've known entrepreneurs who are so capable and so committed to their business, who work so hard and address challenges head on, doing all the right things... only to find their hair falling out in large clumps, their skin erupting in uncomfortable and unsightly rashes or sores, and suffering from gastrointestinal paroxysms that seem to have no cause.

There is a cause: overwork along with prolonged and repeated stress. Your body is in a constant state of fight or flight, putting you at risk for chronic stress-related conditions, autoimmune-like disorders, and heart disease.

The resolution requires an awareness of what's going on in your body, connecting it to how you're behaving in your business, and a willingness to interrupt that connection.

Taking a break – a real break – with no smartphone or email, indeed no laptop or computer, is necessary if you want to truly interrupt that connection.

Your right brain is the creative, feeling part of you and it needs a little breathing space. This is when you can actually recharge your batteries and let your fight-flight-freeze system stand down.

Here are two approaches to taking breaks. The first is to move your body, which helps your brain work better.

- Do walk and talk meetings. Get out of the office.
- Try desk yoga. Every hour or so, stand up and stretch your arms to the ceiling. Bend down and touch your toes. Turn side to side in your chair and twist your spine.
- Take five-minute breaks – no calls, no email – and just breathe. Inhale to a count of four, hold for two, exhale for six.

The second way to take a break is to go on an actual vacation.

- It doesn't have to be costly! Try a staycation, where you 'go away' without going far from home.
- Put your email and smartphone away.
- Read books, watch movies.
- Let your right brain play – pull out your guitar or your paints or your scrapbook.

> *If it's no break at all, it has counter effects. The smartphone negates the break, the family resents your absence, you feed your guilt machine which further exacerbates the stress cycle.*
>
> Cynthia Barlow, C3 Conversations

The New Recipe for Self-Care

Essentially you need to add yet another important job to your long list of responsibilities: director of self-care. Your body and your business will love you for it.

Gather your big ideas and put them in a bowl with your small pockets. Add your long to-do lists a few at a time, alternating with your lack of help, stirring gently. Set aside. In a separate container, insert some breaks into your 12- to 18-hour days. Monitor your brain and your body. As needed insert larger and longer breaks – aka vacations – and keep the earthquake breakdown blues at bay.

26

Break Free

TIME TO SELL?

I t's one of the most important decisions you will make. And the hardest. Is it time for you to break free, to exit stage left? To say goodbye to your business and hello to freedom, your next big thing, and possibly to financial independence? There are a few unmistakable signs that it is indeed the right time for you and the business to move on.

You

A successful run and natural progression, like retirement, may be the impetus for your exit. It may be that all your goals have been met. In which case, you've prepared for this moment and you're likely ready.

Perhaps you've done such a bang-up job that the needs of the business have outgrown what you can reasonably provide. In which case, it's time for someone else to take the helm.

You could also be encountering one of these reasons:

- You're no longer having fun.
- Your business growth has stalled.
- You've come to despise hiring, firing, and paperwork.
- You're frazzled, stressed, and your health is suffering (aka the earthquake breakdown blues).
- There's conflict (or divorce) between partners.
- You don't have enough working capital to continue.
- The death of a business partner has forced your hand.

The Business

Just because it is the right time for *you* to exit doesn't mean it's actually the right time. You'll want to make sure the business and the market environments are also in the right space.

If you're having a tough time, your business may be unhappy and unhealthy too. Before you break free and make your exit, your business should be in great shape, with:

- strong sales and well-performing products and services
- a competent management team
- well defined, repeatable and documented processes
- demonstrable history of profitability
- solid customer base, and
- a plan for continued growth.

It may seem counterintuitive, but the best time to sell your business is when it is doing better than ever.

The Environment

Market conditions, technology, and the regulatory environment can all affect your business and your exit strategy. Here are some questions to ask.

- How many other businesses are for sale in your area or market? Too many (a buyer's market) and it may drive down your price or make it hard to find a buyer.
- What's happening with the economy? Will prospective buyers be able to access financing? Have corporate downsizings increased the number of potential new business owners looking for their next career?
- Are there regulatory changes on the horizon that will positively or negatively affect your business?
- Is new or developing technology going to be a threat or an advantage?

Preparing to Exit

Whether your plan is to sell, transfer, or merge, there are key activities to undertake to ensure you're prepared and to position your business to command top dollar.

Boost profits.

All of a sudden your tax strategy will shift. Rather than low profits to reduce tax payable, when readying your business to sell you want to leave as much money in the business as possible. Prospective buyers want to see strong financial performance and profits.

Clean house.

Polish up the balance sheet, ensure all taxes are paid, discontinue products or services that aren't doing well, review and prune any fringe benefits that are too generous, and be sure you have a few of years worth of audited financial statements.

Work with an advisor.

You'll want someone with experience in your industry and with the exit strategy you're employing. They, along with your accountant, should also be able to help you with a business valuation to establish a reasonable price tag for your business.

If your business is in decline, it may not be valuable enough for someone else to acquire. You may simply decide to liquidate inventory and close your doors.

Regardless, how and when to exit your business is a significant decision that deserves careful thought and planning. Whatever the circumstances, engage your attitude and beliefs to focus on the big picture and its upside.

You're still in the drivers' seat and in control of your own destiny. Everything you've put into your business has led you to this point, and whether or not there's big money attached, you're ready to *break free*.

$$x = y^2$$

Conclusion

There's a catch 22 when you're running your own business. The catch is this: no one knows better than you what needs to be done and how to do it best. After all, this business is your idea. It began with your urge to create or accomplish something. You're probably the best with the clients, the best at putting together sales proposals, and the best one to deal with your international manufacturing partners or your tax accountant.

While you're busy doing some or all of the above, what's happening? Two things: you do not have a high level strategic view of what's going on in your business, and your team isn't fulfilled. In order to lift the ceiling on your growth and success potential, you must stop doing everything yourself.

We're talking about working *on* your business instead of working *in* your business. You've likely heard the phrase before. The truth of the matter is that you will not be able to grow and thrive until you step back and let others do what they do best, while you focus on what you need to do as the leader of the business.

Which option will you choose? Stay at ground zero to master all the tasks? Or let go of the tasks – which others can do – to free yourself up to focus on the strategic direction of your small business?

There's a tipping point beyond which it no longer makes sense for you to 'save money' by continuing to bury your head in the books, or the back end of the website, by doing all your hiring yourself and by serving your customers directly. Continuing on this path means you'll grow only to the limits of your personal abilities.

If, instead, you set the tone, you create the culture and hire the team to do all those things, and you let them loose, then you're free to leverage the abilities of the *whole team* for growth well beyond what you're capable of alone.

Even if you are the whole team, this should serve as a reminder that you, too, need to step back and take a long view of where you're going. Keeping an eye on the business from 30,000 feet lets you ensure all the moving parts are working in harmony. It means you're pulling the strings from above instead of getting bounced around at the bottom of someone else's strings. You be the puppet master, not the puppet.

In Review

In Step One, The Groundwork, you learned the key attributes of working as an independent professional (an iPro) or entrepreneur and how to come up with a great business idea. You read about the importance of identifying your purpose and how to decide on the right legal structure. You explored what it takes to write a winning business plan, how to protect your intellectual property, and why and how to set up the systems that will support your future success. You know about building and updating your business website and how to make sure you've got the right players on the team.

In Step Two, Mine Your Quarry, you explored business culture and how to build one that fuels success rather than snuffs it out. You absorbed a dose of healthy cash-flow management and how to leverage technology. You're more comfortable with hiring and decision making and you even understand the importance of meetings – when handled properly.

In Step Three, To the Moon, you discovered the key elements of growing your business, starting with how to decide if growth is what you want. It isn't for everyone and it might not be for you. You have a better understanding of some of the strategies to help you boost productivity. You can now assess your client or customer roster and know how to tell when it's time to break up with bad ones. You're informed about brand content, marketing, and trade shows. And you know why you might want to write a book. You're also familiar with the signs that it's time to take a break and recharge. And you've got the tools to help you figure out when it might be time to exit your business.

It needn't be complicated, this running your own business. But it is to be taken seriously. How well you handle the business end will have a definite impact on your income, your livelihood, and your experience of life.

We hope that the stories, suggestions, advice, and guidelines in this book leave you feeling ready to *Rock Your Business*.

Leave a review?

Thanks for reading! If you found value in the book and have a minute to spare, we would really appreciate it if you could leave an honest review on Amazon. This helps new readers decide if our book is right for them.

About the Authors

We've been there, done that. We know how to start, run and grow a small business, or an independent entrepreneurial endeavour. We've also thrived as freelancers.

We found ourselves at a point between businesses, between gigs, and we realized we had an opportunity to do something completely different. Something we'd always wanted. For Boni, that was to be utterly self-sufficient and geographically independent. For John, it was to own and live aboard a sailboat. So, we did it. We sold our stuff (like, all of it), packed up a few bags and our two cats and bade adieu to our home, friends and family in Canada. We headed south to a warmer climate and a huge unknown. We bought a 40-foot sailboat, named her *Ingenium*, and have been living aboard somewhere off the Pacific coast of Mexico for a few years.

When we made the move, we had a few freelance clients that followed us, thankfully, but otherwise we had no guaranteed source of income. Our pensions hadn't kicked in yet because we were still too young. (ARE still too young!) But we knew it was right. We knew that following our hearts and trusting our instincts meant a

rare opportunity to create a life, an experience, that many people only dream of.

We didn't know then that our next big thing would be Ingenium Books, our new indie publishing company. But we did create the space for it to present itself to us, when the time was right. It is a creative endeavour that leverages our business experience and our drive to help others. And it led to this book, which does the same thing. We visualize success before it happens and we don't fret when we encounter a failure. We keep our eyes on what we want and aren't surprised when it pretty much happens.

We embrace the global nature of work today and write for the iPro and small business audiences wherever they choose to be in the world. We have researched the statistics and the stories from the U.S., the U.K., the E.U., and Australia. But we are Canadians, from Canada, and the particular brand of English we use throughout the book is Canadian English. Much like today's global economy, Canadian English has been adapted from British roots, heavily influenced by its powerful U.S. neighbour to the south, and recognized around the world for its kindness and generosity.

Boni Wagner-Stafford

Boni is an author, writer, ghostwriter, and editor who has always been *breathing life into language*. She's ghostwritten and/or edited for clients in the finance, business, and health and wellness industries. She is at work on forthcoming nonfiction books of her own, including *The Trauma Trigger* and *The Fibromyalgia Breakthrough*. She's a member of the Alliance of Independent Authors (ALLi) and the Nonfiction Writers Association.

As a Canadian award-winning television reporter, news anchor, producer, and talk show host, working under the names *Boni Fox* and *Boni Fox Gray*, Boni covered politics, government, health, tragedy, victory, First Nations issues, organized crime, fires, floods, and extreme weather. She won several Canadian Association of Broadcaster (CAB) awards and a Jack Webster Award for best documentary.

Boni also held senior management roles in the Ontario government, responsible for media relations and strategic communications planning. There she worked on, or was responsible for, subnational budget documents, policy white papers, and other public-facing reports.

Boni has been at the controls of a helicopter, canoed in the wild backcountry of Northern Ontario, jumped out of an airplane (twice), been skiing in the Rocky Mountains, and hitchhiked across British Columbia. Boni has moved more than 50 times, living in 15 different cities/towns in Canada and Mexico and now resides full-time on her sailboat, *Ingenium*, where she can move on a whim.

John Wagner-Stafford

John is an accomplished creative project producer who has created, served, managed, led, produced, sold, played, performed, recorded, sung, coached, presented, patented, and launched.

Creating a better world is John's personal purpose. As an entrepreneur, change, growth, spontaneity, and improvisation are important tools John uses to compete and succeed in business.

John's creative entrepreneur accomplishments include professional musician (saxophone, vocals); recording engineer with artists like Peter Frampton, Celine Dion, Pat Metheny, and Leonard Cohen; soundtrack producer for film and television; trainer and coach to the sound mixer team at MSNBC when the New York-based network went live for the first time in 1997; producer of notable video games such as Prince of Persia, Myst IV-Revelation, and Splinter Cell IV-Double Agent; COO during the startup phase for franchised brand KANDY Outdoor Flooring Inc., where he designed and built KANDY's first proprietary, integrated sales proposal and customer relationship management (CRM) system; licensed realtor in two Canadian provinces; a master canoeist; and ASA-certified sailor.

To learn more about Ingenium Books:

www.ingeniumbooks.com
hello@ingeniumbooks.com

Acknowledgments

To Canada, for giving us a national identity and frame of reference for everything we do, and ex-pat respect everywhere we go. To our parents, the Wagners and the Staffords, for the wisdom and support as we continued to boldly go where no one in their right minds would.

We are grateful for the career and business opportunities afforded us by so many. In particular, we thank Kelly and Doug Niessen for including us in the startup journey of KANDY Outdoor Flooring. The lessons were invaluable.

Thanks to David Reeve, Molly Billings, Richard Wagner, Kelly Niessen, Ladey Adey, John Newell, and Colin Campbell for reading early versions of this manuscript and providing outstanding feedback. And thanks to Stephen Teatro for sharing your photography skills.

If *Rock Your Business* was born out of our own experience, it was nurtured, watered and fed with thanks to Troy Media, a Canadian content distributor to more than 1800 media outlets. In early 2016, the publisher and CEO of Troy Media asked us if we'd be interested in writing a series of columns for small business and entrepreneurs.

Over the course of a year we published 24 columns. These form the basis of the chapters in this book. We've expanded and adapted them to serve the needs of a global audience rather than solely a Canadian one.

We interviewed nearly two dozen small business leaders who told us their stories and shared their expertise. Their stories helped give life to the lessons we're passing on. Where we needed to close some gaps, we created fictional people and scenarios to demonstrate a point. Want to know who is real and who is a product of our overactive imaginations? We acknowledge and appreciate the following people who shared their time and their experiences as we interviewed them for a column or for the book. In order of appearance:

Vince Fowler, Vested Interest Group
www.vestedinterestgroup.com

Kelly Niessen, KANDY Outdoor Flooring
www.kandyoutdoorflooring.com

David Reeve, Unleash Culture
www.unleashculture.com

Bill Crysler, Furtney Crysler LLP
www.fc-llp.com

Arlene Anderson, Business Advice
www.business-advice.com

Lynn Williams, The Lifestyle Protector
www.lifestyleprotector.ca

Valentine Lovekin, Lovekin Law

www.lovekinlaw.com

Dr. Gabriella Chan, Yocto Law
www.yoctolaw.com

Robert Irani, (formerly of) Bennett Jones
www.bennettjones.com

Dara Sklar, Synced With Dara
www.syncedwithdara.com

Farid Dordar, Perfect Mind
www.perfectmind.com

Tim Morton, Prompta Consulting Group
www.promptaconsultinggroup.com

Sarah Picciotto, OnPoint Legal Research
www.onpointlaw.com

Almira Bardai, Jive PR & Digital
www.jiveprdigital.com

Sharon Ranson, The Ranson Group
www.theransongroup.com

Gary Prenevost, The Franchise Expert
www.canadafranchiseexpert.ca

Ravi Dindayal, Business Development Bank of Canada
www.bdc.ca

Ilan Cooley, LoudMouth Communications

www.loudmouthcommunications.com

Ellen Varner, E-Trademark Universe
www.e-trademarkuniverse.com

Kathy McDonald, Extreme Outdoor Safaris
www.extremeoutdoorsafaris.com

Colin Campbell, ClickSimpleMarketing
www.clicksimplemarketing.com

Cynthia Barlow, C3 Conversations Inc.
www.c3conversations.com

End Notes

"2014 Global Customer Service Barometer: Market Comparison of Findings." American Express, 2011. http://about.americanexpress.com/news/docs/2014x/2014-Global-Customer-Service-Barometer-US.pdf

Anastasi, Tom. *The Successful Entrepreneur: American Dream Done Right.* Glenbridge Publishing, 2010.

Beesley, Caron. "Starting a Freelance Business – How to Take Care of Legal, Tax and Contractual Paperwork." U.S. Small Business Administration 2012 https://www.sba.gov/blogs/starting-freelance-business-how-take-care-legal-tax-and-contractual-paperwork

Business Development Bank of Canada. *Productivity Matters: Benchmarking Your Company to Up Your Game* and *Master Your Cash Flow.* BDC, 2016

Cooper, Steve. "The Government Definition of Small Business is B.S." Forbes, 2012. https://www.forbes.com/sites/stevecooper/2012/09/20/the-government-definition-of-small-business-is-b-s/#5151081e360a

"Digital Disconnect in Customer Engagement: Companies Need to Rebalance Digital and Traditional Investments to Drive Growth." Accenture Strategy, 2016. https://www.accenture.com/us-en/insight-digital-disconnect-customer-engagement

"Does Disruption Drive Job Creation?" EY Global Job Creation Survey, 2016. http://www.ey.com/Publication/vwLUAssets/ey-job-creation-survey-2016

Hoomans, Dr. Joel. "35,000 Decisions: The Great Choices of Strategic Leaders." Roberts Wesleyan College, 2015. https://go.roberts.edu/leadingedge/the-great-choices-of-strategic-leaders

"Key Small Business Statistics." Government of Canada, 2016. https://www.ic.gc.ca/eic/site/061.nsf/eng/h_03018.html
Klein, Gary. *The Power of Intuition*. Random House, 2004.

Konings, Jozef and Vanormelingen, Stijn. "The Impact of Training on Productivity and Wages: Firm Level Evidence." IZA Discussion Paper No. 4731. Available at SSRN: https://ssrn.com/abstract=1549207

Leighton, P., and Brown, D. "Future Working: The rise of Europe's Independent Professionals (iPros). Report of the European Forum of Independent Professionals, 2013.

McBean, Marnie. *The Power of More: How Small Steps Can Help You Achieve Big Goals*. Greystone Books, 2012.

Morris, Tricia. "13 Shocking Customer Service Statistics." *Parature Customer Service Success Blog, 2015*. http://www.parature.com/13-customer-service-statistics/

OECD (2017). *"Self-employment Rate* (indicator)." doi: 10.1787/fb58715e-en

Reeve, David. *Unleash Culture: How to Design, Implement & Sustain a*

Powerful Culture That Accelerates the Growth of Your Brand. Norseman Books, 2016.

Reichheld, Fred. "Measuring Your Net Promoter Score." Net Promoter System. http://www.netpromotersystem.com/speaking-engagements/fred-reichheld.aspx

"Self-employment, Historical Summary." Statistics Canada, 2017. http://www.statcan.gc.ca/tables-tableaux/sum-som/l01/cst01/labor64-eng.htm

Tucker, Robert. *Driving Growth Through Innovation*, and *Seven Strategies for Generating Business Ideas*. Berrett-Koehler Publishers, 2008.

Wansink, Brian and Sobal, Jeffery. "Mindless Eating: The 200 Daily Food Decisions We Overlook." *Environment and Behavior*, Vol 39, Issue 1, July 2016, pp. 106 - 123 10.1177/0013916506295573

Ward, Matthew & Rhodes, Chris. "Small Business and the UK Economy." U.K. Parliament, 2014. researchbriefings.files.parliament.uk/documents/SN06078/SN06078.pdf

WELLS, TINA. "Millennials are Here... and They're Entrepreneurial". Buzz Marketing Group, 2014. http://buzzmg.com/2014/08/08/millennials-are-here-and-theyre-entrepreneurial/

Also by Boni Wagner-Stafford

Kitty Karma: Big Stories of Small Cats Who Change Our Lives (editor and contributing author)

WANTED: How to Create a Relationship That Really Works (editor)

No More Author Envy: 9 Essential Steps to Writing Your First Book (author)

www.ingramcontent.com/pod-product-compliance
Lightning Source LLC
Chambersburg PA
CBHW071228210326
41597CB00016B/1983